# Vita Sapien
## A Sustainable Life Philosophy
### Guy Lane

Vita Sapien
A Sustainable Life Philosophy
Guy Lane

ISBN: 979-8-268-36462-0

Published in Australia
A Vita Sapien Publication
March 2026

All internal images are copyright © Guy Lane or appropriately referenced.

Order copies:
vitaeplaneta@gmail.com

Paperback trim size: 4" x 6"

vitasapien.org

# Our Predicament ..................................... 1
## Introduction ............................................. 1
## A Tale of Two Tribes ............................... 5
## According to the Science ..................... 31
## Material View ....................................... 46
## Vita Sapien Cosmology ........................ 68

# Ecosystem Spirituality ........................ 73
## Gya ....................................................... 74
## Four Dimensions .................................. 82
## Eight Themes ....................................... 88
## Experience & Practice ........................ 116
## Imagine Reflourishing ........................ 121

# The Transition ..................................... 130
## The Verdant Age ................................. 131
## Changing Trajectory ........................... 134

# Vita Practice ........................................ 140
## Fostering Mass-Ecophany .................. 141
## Earthwork ........................................... 144

| | |
|---|---|
| **Vita Quests** | **145** |
| **Being Vitan** | **175** |
| **Resources** | **181** |
| **About ViSO** | **181** |
| **The Quenn** | **182** |
| **Glossary** | **186** |
| **About the Author** | **196** |
| **Contact ViSO** | **198** |
| **Comments From Readers** | **198** |

A Sustainable Life Philosophy

# Our Predicament

## Introduction

I am an environmental scientist, and for three decades I have been watching humanity degrade the Living Planet, our life support system. My enduring question has been: 'Why?'

Why not instead foster a civilization and ecosystem that thrives?

# Vita Sapien

In August 2016 it became clear to me that the root of our man-made crisis was that most people hold unsustainable worldviews.

The term *worldview* relates to how a person sees and understands the world in which they live. People view life framed by their beliefs (religion & spirituality), their knowledge, (including scientific understanding), the culture of their society, and their own personal experiences. No two worldviews are alike, although many share common themes.

The inspiration for this book was to frame a worldview that gives humanity the best chance of surviving the 21st Century and thriving beyond. This is achieved primarily through the fusion of environmental science and spirituality grounded in the living world – put another way, *eco-science & ecosystem spirituality*.

# A Sustainable Life Philosophy

Vita Sapien Philosophy gains deeper meaning when considered alongside six valuable traditions.

Of particular note are Indigenous Worldviews which represent humanity's original and unbroken spiritual connection to nature, unchanged since the Cognitive Revolution 70,000 years ago.

Other traditions that offer complementary wisdom to Vita Sapien Philosophy include: Stoicism, Buddhism, Taoism, Shinto, and Western Eco-spirituality.

I believe that a sustainable life philosophy written for the times could foster behavioural changes that could alter the trajectory of human civilization.

Instead of heading toward the abyss, we could move toward a Verdant Age, where humanity and the Living Planet thrive in synergy deep into the Long Future.

# Vita Sapien

This book has five Parts.

- Our Predicament
- Spiritual Renaturing
- The Transition
- Vita Practice
- Resources

The first chapter **Our Predicament** outlines where we are with respect to the global crisis that Vita Sapien Philosophy seeks to resolve.

**Spiritual Renaturing** introduces the spiritual belief in Gya, Ecosystem Spirituality, and the *Vita Spiritual Framework* that makes it easy to understand *the subject* of spirituality and see how it applies to sustainability.

**The Transition** details the Verdant Age—the aspirational future where humans and the Living Planet thrive in harmony—and the transition plan to get there.

**Vita Practice** describes ways in which individuals can give effect to this sustainable

## A Sustainable Life Philosophy

life philosophy and help advance the Verdant Age. This includes twelve practices referred to as Quests.

Finally, **Resources** introduces Vita Sapien Organisation—the institution behind the philosophy—and how you can support and get involved.

In an hour or so when you come to the end of this book, I ask that you sit in quiet contemplation and ask yourself a single question:

"What should I do with
the rest of my life?"

Guy Lane – 16 March, 2026

# A Tale of Two Tribes

Today around 8.2 billion humans—*Homo sapiens*—call the Living Planet their home. It is believed that the *Homo sapiens* evolved around 300,000 years ago, descendants of

# Vita Sapien

*Homo Heidelbergensis.*
Evidence suggests that the early *Homo sapiens* differed little in their behaviour from their forebears. However, around 70,000 years ago, a dramatic shift in *Homo sapiens'* cognition occurred. So profound was this 'awakening' that it is known by the grand title: the *Cognitive Revolution*.

To grasp how profound was this change, imagine a hypothetical conversation between two tribes, one of which has undergone this cognitive transformation and the other hasn't. This wouldn't have happened in real life, but the scenario helps us understand the profound results of the Cognitive Revolution.

Two tribes meet on the bank of a river. The grass is tall and lush. The air is warm and alive with the sounds of insects and birds. It is high season, and there is a lot of food in the environment, so there is nothing much to compete over. The two clans sit down to talk.

# A Sustainable Life Philosophy

River Mussel clan are new to the area, having slowly moved their way in from the South. They are chatty and have a lot to say.

The clan leader points to his people one-by-one. He describes the archer, the one who makes bows and arrows. He points to the needle maker who can sew form-fitting clothing. Others in his clan specialise in finding minerals to paint with, and medicinal plants. Others are expert in shaping complex stone tools.

River Mussel clan stand-out in these parts because of the sophistication of their tools, the extent of their vocabulary. They are known for the detail and beauty of their artworks left behind on the walls of caves, carried with them as tiny statues, or worn as jewellery or facial paint. They have an advanced spiritual perception and beliefs about what happens to a person after death.

The other clan is called Heavy Stone. Their people have been in this region for thousands of years. They have little to say because they know only few words and their minds aren't sharp enough to form complex thoughts. They can't really plan, so they have not mastered archery, and they hunt with just sharpened stones on the end of sticks. The landscape offers less for them to eat. They lack sewn clothing, and the extent of their artistry is feathers in their hair, and a handful of coloured stones.

In our hypothetical, when Heavy Stone bury their dead, that's all they do. They dig a hole, push the body in, and cover it over. River Mussel Clan, on the other hand, have extensive funerary practices which involve burying the dead with artefacts in specific locations and with rituals involved.

While this encounter is imagined, the profound impact of the Cognitive Revolution is laid bare.

One might think that these two clans were from a different species. But they are both

# A Sustainable Life Philosophy

*Homo sapiens*. A primary difference between them is that a metaphorical switch was flicked to the 'On' position inside the minds of the River Mussel clan, and this opened a reservoir of intellect, curiosity, symbolism, innovation, and spirituality.

All these things are interconnected, intertwined, interlinked, inseparable, and from the same source.

Let us call these mental faculties *Thinking-Feeling* and view them as an emergent property of a complex central nervous system that arose through a subtle evolution in the wiring of the brain, and the advancement of language and culture.

Some may experience these insights as external gifts or divine inspiration. Vita Sapien Philosophy understands them as emergent properties of our remarkable central nervous systems—which are themselves components of the long evolutionary journey of the living planet of which we are a part. Either way, the capacity for insight and spiritual experience is real and valuable.

The Cognitive Revolution fostered a matrix of intellectual and transcendent abilities. These created pathways for engineering, mathematics, complex tool production, rich language, symbolic representation, art, funerary practice, stories and shared beliefs, and the full expression of what we now know as spirituality.

Vita Sapien Philosophy holds that 'cognition' relates to knowing, understanding, and awareness—encompassing intellectual functions such as reasoning, memory, and perception, as well as reflective and contemplative capacities that allow for spiritual insight, meaning-making, and inner growth.

These new cognitive abilities conferred huge advantage to the 'modern' humans, making it easier for them to both compete and cooperate, to communicate, to find food and shelter, and to survive a wider set of climatic conditions.

The revolution of the mind is believed to have begun in Africa around 70,000 years ago. Eventually these Thinking-Feeling people found their way to Europe 40,000 years ago, people we now know as the Cro-Magnon or Early European Modern Humans.

The capacity for Thinking-Feeling is the origin of the full expression of spirituality in humans, as evidenced by the cave paintings and the funerary practices of the Cro-Magnon people.

# Spirituality

All human beings have spirituality. Think of it as the perception of being part of a greater thing, a quest for answers to imponderable questions, the ability to fall periodically into transcendent mental states, the awareness of mortality, and holding a view of what comes after life ends.

## Vita Sapien

In its original form, human spirituality is associated with nature: with landscapes, seasons, wildlife, plants, insects, rivers, and coastlines.

However, spirituality is a vessel that can hold many different types of belief. The hunter-gatherer lifestyles of the Cro-Magnon gave way to agricultural communities as the Ice Age ended and the climatically stable Holocene Epoch began around 12,000 years ago. As human culture changed, so did the spiritual expression of those people.

Later, in a period referred to as the Axial Age —around 2,300 to 2,800 years ago—a new suite of beliefs spread around the world and severed humanity spiritually from nature. Most of the religions and spiritual philosophies that exist today have their origins in the Axial Age.

For the vast majority of human existence since the Cognitive Revolution—tens of thousands of years—human spirituality was

## A Sustainable Life Philosophy

intimately connected to the natural world. Only in the last few thousand years has the dominant spiritual expression has been *denatured*.

As a result of the behaviours that these denatured beliefs inspire, our planetary life-support system is in decline.

'Decline' is a profound understatement. Human civilization is spiralling towards self-extinction, dragging most life on Earth with us. We have devastated the climate and ecological system of our home planet, and there is nowhere else to go.

Make no mistake, we are in a crisis of humanity—a climate and ecological crisis—and nothing short of a radical transformation will save us.

Imagine a dozen people in a rubber raft heading for deadly rapids. If there is competent leadership and everyone cooperates some people may survive to raft another day. Alternatively, they all perish in the churning water.

Translating this to real life, we need a revolution in the way that humans relate to the Living Planet, and this necessarily begins with a spiritual transformation. A return to our innate, nature spirituality. This transformation doesn't require abandoning modernity—it requires reorienting it toward life rather than consumption and growth.

Absent this transformation, humanity and most life on Earth will likely perish in the not-too-distant future. Global heating and ecosystem destruction together with the toxification of nature (you have microplastic in your brain) are the primary drivers of this impending collapse.

A pathway to restore our Living Planet to full health is *Spiritual Renaturing*—a global spiritual reconnection with nature, and the acceptance of knowledge and practice that can guide us through the troubled times ahead.

# A Sustainable Life Philosophy

The first *Homo sapiens* to arrive in Europe, the Cro-Magnon, arrived during a warm period that followed an ice age. As the next ice age came on, the Cro-Magnon adapted and survived.

Today, a climactic change is occurring. The period of ice ages is in the past. Now the future is one of warming, then overheating, and potentially an annihilating hothouse.

A new culture is possible in this changing climate, a culture that views the world through a lens that provides the best opportunity to survive what's coming and thrive thereafter.

By selecting the spiritual and intellectual tools that work, Vita Sapien Philosophy curates the mindset that will help us survive this century and thrive beyond.

## Spiritual Marketplace

One hundred years ago in the West, if you wanted spirituality, you went to the Church.

# Vita Sapien

Today's spiritual marketplace is radically diverse. Walk into a shop selling metaphysical and New Age supplies and you'll find ancient religious traditions (Christianity, Buddhism, Islam, Hinduism), wellness practices (yoga, meditation, Tai Chi), and New Age eclecticism (crystals, tarot, channeling). Some offerings have deep philosophical roots; others are recent inventions or fringe theories.

Many pursuits—from sports to hobbies to traditional practices—similarly fill our spiritual needs and provide genuine meaning for many. These pursuits nourish the spiritual dimension of our lives, give us a sense of meaning, and can open pathways to transcendence.

Most spiritual traditions weren't designed to address the climate and ecological crisis. This isn't a failing—most were developed long before planetary-scale environmental collapse was conceivable. But it does create a gap. Our civilization and global ecosystem are heading

## A Sustainable Life Philosophy

toward the abyss, and we need spiritual frameworks that speak to this reality.

Many of us have become so immersed in modern life—its activities, technologies, and distractions—that we've lost the ability to hear what the natural world is telling us. The signals are there, but our culture hasn't taught us to recognise them.

As a result, most people have no sense that our Living Planet is dying and that if she dies, we die with her.

There is a powerful article titled *Drowning Doesn't Look Like Drowning* by coast guard Mario Vittone. He says that most people don't know what a drowning person looks like. We think that they wave their arms, shouting, "Help! Help!" like they do on TV.

However, the *Instinctive Drowning Response* isn't like that. Drowning is a 'deceptively quiet event'. Drowning people look peaceful, and this explains why so many perish in the water just a short distance from family and friends.

Similarly, most people don't know what a dying planet looks like, even though we are living on one. People cannot feel that the planet is dying because we are spiritually disconnected from nature.

Vita Sapien Philosophy proposes that we augment our spiritual views to include a reverence, a passion, and a deep love for nature. A fascination for nature. A spiritual bond to our beautiful Living Planet.

Because of the relationship between spirituality and behaviour, when people undergo spiritual change, they are primed for behavioural change. And this is exactly what we need in order to change the trajectory of human civilization away from the abyss.

Nature spirituality fosters moral concern for nature, and this is the most direct pathway to

# A Sustainable Life Philosophy

creating right action to make things better for our planet and our future.

Pro-environmental behavioural change can be brought about in people when spiritual enlightenment to nature is paired with a deeper understanding of how nature works, and guidance for right action.

When people align their hearts, minds, and efforts to the wellbeing of nature—our planetary life support system—the trajectory of human civilization can shift away from the extinction abyss toward a future, environmentally sustainable civilization: the Verdant Age. Vita Sapien Philosophy seeks to enable this transformation.

Around the world there are millions of people who possess three core characteristics:

- A deep love and reverence for nature (Vita Sapien frames this as a spiritual connection)

## Vita Sapien

- Trust in scientific consensus on major issues
- Willingness to take action for environmental causes

Vita Sapien Philosophy calls these people Vitans—Life People. Not everyone starts as a Vitan. Many people are *Proto-Vitans*—demonstrating one or two of these characteristics. Perhaps they care deeply about nature but distrust science, or trust science but haven't yet felt a spiritual connection to the Living Planet.

A coherent philosophy is needed for people to become agents of transformation taking expedient action for the Living Planet.

A spiritual connection to nature is essential. What do the dominant spiritual philosophies offer on this subject?

A Sustainable Life Philosophy

# Worldviews & Sustainability

You may be surprised to learn that the dominant spiritual and philosophical worldviews of today offer little of practical use to reconnect us to nature and to resolve the *Anthropocene Crisis*.

The Anthropocene is a scientific name for the modern era in which humans are the main drivers of change in the climate and environment. Originally a geological term, it now broadly describes our current era of human-dominated planetary change.

For Vita Sapien Philosophy, the term Anthropocene Crisis describes the interconnected matrix of global problems including climate change, ecological collapse, microplastic contamination, nuclear threat, and related challenges. Others refer to the polycrisis or metacrisis—different terms for essentially the same phenomenon.

## Vita Sapien

While some spiritual traditions offer useful advice regarding the Anthropocene Crisis, many do not.

Today's spiritual landscape among eight billion humans is dominated by a few major traditions, with Christianity (31%), Islam (24%), and Hinduism (15%) representing the majority. Significantly, 16% identify as non-religious.

Most of the spiritual traditions on the list are grounded in Axial Age beliefs and include the Abrahamic religions (Christianity, Islam, and Judaism), Hinduism, Buddhism, Taoism, etc.

The point to make here is that these spiritual traditions were conceived over 2,000 years before the Anthropocene even began. It is therefore no surprise that climate change and global ecosystem collapse are not referred to in the founding documents. The question is whether these traditions can be reinterpreted to address planetary-scale crises.

# A Sustainable Life Philosophy

This concern is particularly relevant in the West. Carl Safina in his book *Alfie and Me: What Owls Know, What Humans Believe* explores how different cultures relate to nature. He examines how certain philosophical ideas—including Platonic dualism between material and spiritual realms—became embedded in Western thought and contributed to viewing nature as separate from the sacred.

These ideas emerged when Earth's human population was a fraction of today's, and wilderness seemed boundless. Now, with over 8 billion people and rapid ecological decline, we need a philosophy specifically designed for planetary-scale crisis and transition to a sustainable civilization.

A legitimate concern is whether some interpretations of End Times beliefs—such as certain readings of Christianity's Armageddon, Islam's Qiyamah, or Hinduism's Kali Yuga—might discourage environmental action by framing ecological decline as inevitable or divinely ordained. However, many practitioners within these traditions are actively developing ecological theologies and finding environmental imperatives within their faiths.

The challenge isn't abandoning these traditions, but ensuring they speak powerfully to our current emergency. When they do, mainstream religion becomes a powerful ally in advancing the Verdant Age.

## Six Valuable Worldviews

With respect to addressing the Anthropocene Crisis, there is value in some spiritual / philosophical traditions.

Six in particular stand out:

- Buddhism
- Taoism
- Shinto
- Stoicism

# A Sustainable Life Philosophy

- Western Eco-spirituality
- Indigenous Worldview

Not all of what is written in these philosophies is resonant with Vita Sapien. However, some of the gems are considered here in brief.

**Buddhism, Taoism, and Shinto** (Japanese folk religion) all have reverence for nature and observance of natural flows.

Buddhism teaches that we should be intimately grounded in reality, and accept that suffering is a normal part of the human condition. Suffering can be reduced by letting go of the need for things we can happily live without. This insight helps us find balance when the world around us is in turmoil. Buddhism teaches *dependent origination*, that all things have a cause, and *karma*, that what we receive in life is a function of what we give.

Taoism teaches that there is a natural way of things—the Tao—and a flow into which we can become entrained like a leaf in a stream. *Wu wei* is the practice of effortless action, doing less, but in harmony with what is natural.

Shinto has the concept of kami—what Vita Sapien refers to as Parasomatic Spirit. Kami holds that some natural features—groves, waterfalls, ancient trees—are imbued with a unique spirit worthy of reverence. The red archway called *Torii* indicates that kami lies beyond and that reverential behaviour ought begin. Shinto is also so tightly interwoven in Japanese life that most people don't identify it as a religion, *per se*, but as a cultural practice. This is precisely the model for how Vita Sapien Philosophy might take root — not as a religion, but as a way of living.

**Stoicism** is an ancient Greek philosophy centred on *Eudaimonia*—living a life that is good for oneself and for society, through virtue, wisdom, and rationality. a daily reminder of our mortality and an invitation to

# A Sustainable Life Philosophy

humility. Stoicism has a central focus on understanding the pragmatic reality of life and not being blindsided by events. When the Emperor Nero ordered Seneca—one of the great Stoic writers—to take his own life, Seneca met his fate with complete composure. This is Stoicism in its purest form: not wishful thinking, but a grounded acceptance of how things actually are. A more contemporary Stoic example is James Stockdale after whom the *Stockdale Paradox* is named, featured later in this book.

**Western Ecospirituality** borrows from many of these traditions and expresses itself through cultural practices such as organic growing, low-consumption living, nature immersion, and environmental activism.

**Indigenous worldview** can be viewed as a continuation of the original thinking-feeling *Homo sapiens*. This worldview is unique among all others in that it identifies the individual as a part of the landscape and the ecosystem.

# Vita Sapien

Some indigenous peoples can trace their lineage back as much as 50,000 years, as in the case of the Aboriginal people of Australia. By contrast, New Zealand Maori culture dates back only about 900 years. Above all, Indigenous worldview carries a deep wisdom of ecological sustainability, accumulated over countless generations—a striking counterpoint to western culture, which has practically bankrupted the global ecosystem in just 300 years since the Industrial Revolution

These Six Valuable Worldviews – Stoicism, Buddhism, Taoism, Shinto, Western Ecospirituality, and Indigenous Worldview—account for around maybe around 15% of the 8.3 billion humans in the world today.

However, even combined, they do not provide us with all the tools we need to effectively resolve the Anthropocene Crisis. Climate and ecological collapse is a crisis of modernity floundering in ancient ideas, so we need some modern ideas in the mix.

# A Sustainable Life Philosophy

The Six Valuable Worldviews make a good starting point for a sustainable life philosophy that is designed specifically to resolve the Anthropocene Crisis in a single human generation.

Vita Sapien Philosophy provides the missing wisdom. Combined with the other worldviews, it is possible to establish a right relationship between humans and nature, a relationship that will endure through this tumultuous century and beyond.

A question arises, "What has philosophy got to do with sustainability?"

Simple. People are motivated to act based on what they know and what they believe. Of the two, beliefs are the greater motivator of action.

If you believe that our Living Planet is sacred, you will nurture her and protect her. Alternatively, if you believe that our Living

## Vita Sapien

Planet is simply a resource to be exploited then you will exploit and destroy her.

If we want people to care for nature – our life support system – we need them to have nature at the heart of their worldview and their spirituality.

The word 'nature' is used extensively in this book, and it has given a specific context.

In Vita Sapien Philosophy, the word 'nature' has a specific definition.

When we speak of nature, we are not referring to black holes and galaxies on the far edge of the observable universe or the quirky interactions of subatomic particles.

Instead, nature refers to living organisms, ecosystems and natural processes that take place within Earth's biosphere, and those factors that influence the biosphere such as the Sun, Moon, climate and weather, and tectonic forces.

## A Sustainable Life Philosophy

Vita Sapien Philosophy offers ideas about how individuals can connect to nature, and in doing so unleash the extraordinary power within each of us to do the audacious things that are necessary to prevent the collapse of the global ecosystem. To be effective, we must be properly advised by the latest science.

# According to the Science

What does modern science tell us about the relationship between humans and our Living Planet? The news is dire—but understanding the full scope of our predicament is essential.

Before examining the evidence, we need the right philosophical frame.

## The Stockdale Paradox

Within the environmental community, two unhelpful extremes dominate:

- Doomerism declares human extinction inevitable, that we've already passed the point of no return, so why bother?

- Techno-optimism assumes we can simply invent our way out of crisis—that solar panels and electric vehicles alone will save us.

Both worldviews increase the likelihood of collapse because they do not incite right action.

The Stockdale Paradox, named after Admiral James Stockdale, offers an alternative perspective that fosters right action.

As the highest-ranking US military officer held in North Vietnamese POW camps, Stockdale survived seven years of imprisonment and torture. He observed that two types of prisoners died first:

- Pessimists lost hope early and gave up.

# A Sustainable Life Philosophy

- Optimists set unrealistic expectations for release (e.g. *We'll be out by Christmas*) and when repeatedly disappointed, fell into despair.

Those who survived held what seemed like contradictory views: unflinching acceptance of their brutal reality combined with unwavering faith they would ultimately prevail.

Vita Sapien Philosophy embraces the Stockdale Paradox. We will confront the brutal facts of our ecological predicament without flinching, whilst maintaining unwavering commitment to advancing the Verdant Age.

The brutal facts: humanity <u>may</u> have already pushed Earth's systems past critical tipping points. Climate and ecological collapse <u>may</u> be inevitable regardless of what we do now.

We must accept this possibility.

And yet: We must do everything in our power to mitigate it and create conditions for life—human and otherwise—to persist and eventually thrive.

This is not contradiction. This is Earth wisdom.

## What the Science Shows

Scientists communicate through peer-reviewed papers published in journals. What follows are summaries of a handful of key papers that reveal where we stand—and what we might learn from them.

Grouped thematically, the papers show:

## What the Living Planet Does:

- Earth as a self-regulating system

## What Humans Have Done:

- Humans as unsustainable superpredators
- The collapse of wildlife

# A Sustainable Life Philosophy

- The dominance of human infrastructure
- The extent of skyglow and loss of starlight

**Where We're Headed:**

- The present trajectory towards the Hothouse
- The damage to fundamental Earth systems needed for life

**The Challenge:**

- The overwhelming complexity of our predicament

Each paper description is followed by implications for how we might respond.

## By and for the Biosphere

Lovelock, James E., and Lynn Margulis. "Atmospheric homeostasis by and for the biosphere: the Gaia hypothesis." Tellus 26.1-2 (1974): 2-10.

## Vita Sapien

This is the paper that introduced the Gaia Hypothesis to the world in 1974.

Written by James Lovelock and Lynn Margulis, the Gaia Hypothesis has a poetic name even though the argument in the paper is grounded in physics, with an emphasis on entropy.

In short, the Gaia Hypothesis says that living organisms have evolved mechanisms to regulate the temperature of planet Earth, to keep it within the range best suited for life to flourish.

Simply put, the Living Planet behaves in the manner of a single organism in that it maintains internal homeostasis.

From the Gaia Hypothesis we can deduce that to maintain a stable climate all we need to do is to restore the climate to its pre-industrial state and ensure that there is an abundance of wilderness on Earth. Gaia provides our planet with an excellent air conditioning system and all we need to do is look after her.

## Unsustainable Super-predators

Darimont, Chris T., et al. "The unique ecology of human predators." Science 349.6250 (2015): 858-860.

Darimont and others found that humans kill adult prey at much higher rates than other predator species. This interferes with the reproductive success of the prey species.

In addition, humans use advanced technology that way outcompetes their rival predators. As such, human hunters and fishers can be regarded as unsustainable super-predators.

Humans have been predators from our earliest days. The advent of archery 70,000 years ago gave humans a major advantage over our competitor predators, and our technology has become increasingly more deadly year by year.

Vita Sapien

Whilst humans may have been super-predators for a long time, not all human cultures are unsustainable in their predation. We need to learn from the sustainable hunters, the indigenous people, about the right relationship between humans and the animals we take for food. Today, for example, the relationship between humans and livestock is way out of balance.

## 4% Wild Mammals

Bar-On, Yinon M., Rob Phillips, and Ron Milo. "The biomass distribution on Earth." Proceedings of the National Academy of Sciences 115.25 (2018): 6506-6511.

Back in the time of River Mussel Clan if you weighed all the mammals on Earth (referred to as mammalian biomass) you would find that humans represented just a tiny fraction of the total, and the balance would be wildlife.

*96% of mammalian biomass is humans and livestock. Just 4% is wildlife.*

# A Sustainable Life Philosophy

Today, the situation is reversed: just 4% of mammalian biomass is wildlife.

This means that there is now 15 times more livestock than wild animals, by mass. This is itself a good reason to adopt a low meat diet.

One of the reasons that wildlife is shrinking is that we have paved the planet and replaced natural habitat with human habitat to such an extent that there is now more stuff than life.

## More Stuff Than Life

Elhacham, Emily, et al. "Global human-made mass exceeds all living biomass." Nature 588.7838 (2020): 442-444.

The findings of this paper are mind-blowing in demonstrating the profound footprint of humanity on our Living Planet.

Over the past century the mass of material produced by humans – the technosphere – doubled every twenty years or so, while the mass of the biosphere remained relatively steady.

## Vita Sapien

In 2020, the mass of the technosphere exceeded the mass of the biosphere for the first time.

There is now more stuff manufactured by humans than there is living matter that grew here.

- There is twice as much plastic on Earth as there are animals
- There are more buildings and infrastructure than trees and shrubs
- Twenty years from now there will be twice as much technosphere

Perhaps we have built enough. We have certainly built enough streetlamps.

## No Stars for You, Tonight

Falchi, Fabio, et al. "The new world atlas of artificial night sky brightness." Science advances 2.6 (2016): e1600377.

Artificial light is another aspect of the technosphere, creating artificial night sky brightness or skyglow. Skyglow is caused by artificial light reflecting off tiny particles in the air and making the night sky glow slightly. This hides the dimmer stars from view.

As a result of skyglow our Milky Way galaxy is invisible to more than one-third of humanity, including 60% of Europeans and nearly 80% of North Americans. In some places like Singapore, the night is never full-dark at night, but a permanent twilight. Skyglow diminishes human flourishing, and it is terrible for wildlife, particularly birds and insects. We need to reduce Skyglow and allow people to contemplate the cosmos that lies above the biosphere. This will also help make things better for wildlife which is under increasing stress from global heating.

## Heading to the Hothouse

Steffen, Will, et al. "Trajectories of the Earth System in the Anthropocene." Proceedings of the National Academy of Sciences 115.33 (2018): 8252-8259.

# Vita Sapien

This iconic paper from 2018 reviews climactic changes from the past to identify patterns and trajectories for the future. It says that if global average temperatures rise, at around 2 degrees Celsius above pre-industrial temperatures we risk triggering 'a cascade of climate tipping points' that will cause temperatures to go higher still, driving Earth onto a 'Hothouse Earth' pathway. This potentially risks 6 degrees Celsius above pre-industrial temperatures, ruinous for human civilization.

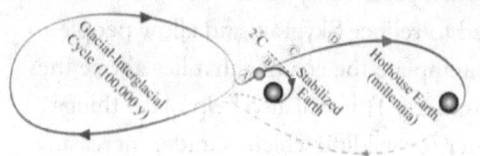

The paper includes a diagram showing an alternative future where humans tackle global heating and stabilise the Earth at or below the 2 degrees Celsius threshold.

A Sustainable Life Philosophy

# Six Boundaries Broken

Richardson, Katherine, et al. "Earth beyond six of nine planetary boundaries." Science advances 9.37 (2023): eadh2458.

There are nine dumb ways to die on planet Earth and we have blundered into seven of them, already.

The Planetary Boundaries framework seeks to identify the key processes that regulate the stability and resilience of the interconnected Earth systems.

In 2023 the framework quantified all boundaries and concluded that six of the nine boundaries have been transgressed.

"Crossing boundaries increases the risk of generating large-scale abrupt or environmental changes."

Each of the Planetary Boundaries are discussed later in the book.

However, a takeaway message is that we need a civilization that honours all nine Planetary Boundaries.

We need civilisation that is Nine-Boundaries Safe.

As if we didn't have enough on our plate as we hurtle to 2°C and beyond, we also have to deal the profound complexity of our predicament.

## Ghastly Complicated

Bradshaw, Corey JA, et al. "Underestimating the challenges of avoiding a ghastly future." Frontiers in Conservation Science 1 (2021): 615419.

This paper holds the following chilling insights: "*…future environmental conditions will be far more dangerous than currently believed. The scale of the threats to the biosphere and all its life-forms – including humanity – is in fact so great that it is difficult to grasp for even well-informed experts.*"

# A Sustainable Life Philosophy

This paper ought to make us immediately leap out of our skins and start doing everything we can to bail-out our sinking ship.

*All-hands-on-deck!*

This is not something for the future 'to do list'. It calls for action, now. We should do the biggest thing we are capable of doing today and do something grander tomorrow. And keep doing that until we die, content in the knowledge that we honoured our responsibility to our Living Planet and the future generations of our own kind.

From the Cognitive Revolution to today's science, we now have a comprehensive picture of our predicament. These ideas form the **Material View**—a framework for understanding humanity's relationship with the Living Planet.

Vita Sapien

# Material View

Material View is a summary of the physical aspects of our global predicament. It is advised mainly by environmental sciences and possible future scenarios.

- Biosphere as Life Support
- *Homo sapiens*
- The Anthropocene
- Planetary Boundaries
- The Long Future
- Worse Than the Permian
- Transition

## Biosphere as Life Support

The word 'biosphere' describes both the place where life exists on Earth, and the totality of life on Earth.

As the name suggests, the shape of the biosphere is a thin-walled sphere, located on the outer surface of our planet. The biosphere includes all the animals, plants, and other living things, plus the ocean, atmosphere, soils, and other substrates that are the habitat of life.

Gaia Theory tells us that animals and plants behave in a manner that maintains the condition of the atmosphere to ensure that the planet doesn't get too hot or cold. Life on Earth maintains conditions suited to the wellbeing of life on Earth.

It is as though all the living things in the biosphere behave in the manner of a single living being that self-regulates its own temperature.

The biosphere self-regulates and thus acts as a life-support system for humanity through a variety of mechanisms. For example, ocean plankton help to create the rain that falls onto our crops; plants produce atmospheric oxygen for us to breathe; plants also produce food, pharmaceuticals and materials like wood, hemp, and cotton.

# Vita Sapien

The biosphere is the life-support system for humans. Destroying the biosphere is a form of collective suicide. And yet, that is exactly what *Homo sapiens* have been doing over the last 80 years or so, the time of the Anthropocene.

## *Homo sapiens*

Human beings are holobionts, which is to say an organism made of many organisms.

Indeed, human bodies contain more non-human cells than human cells. About 60% by number of cells in a human body are microbiome, consisting of bacteria, fungi, archaea, protists, and viruses. The microbiome accounts for about 15% of the human body by mass.

We are, ourselves, an ecosystem. We don't just live in the biosphere; the biosphere lives within us. To recap our evolutionary journey, *Homo sapiens* evolved around 300,000 years ago but it was only about 70,000 years ago

# A Sustainable Life Philosophy

that our central nervous system and language became sophisticated enough for the Thinking-Feeling awakening that fostered innovation, engineering, mathematics, art, culture and spirituality.

The native spiritual expression for humans that sustained us for more than 80% of the last 70,000 years is a connection to wild animals and plants, ecosystems, forests, lakes, shorelines, clouds, storms, and the rain, thunder, and lightning that the storms bring.

This is an organic, innate, natural spiritual expression of the human organism resonating with the ecosystem within and without.

However, from the Axial Age, humans began to synthesise spiritual beliefs that involved Gods, statues, symbols, activities and ultimately machines that run counter to nature.

Today, for example, there is a legion of space-bros who have attached their spiritual locus to rockets and spacecraft. They have become convinced that the frigid, lifeless planet Mars is an alternative home for humanity.

These beliefs underpin behaviours that have a negative effect on the biosphere such as launching rockets adjacent to turtle rookeries and allowing thousands of satellites to burn-up in Earth's atmosphere.

The human footprint on nature is now so profound that the entire global ecosystem is in severe decline, placing billions of humans and millions of species at risk of extinction in the coming years and decades.

Much of this harm has been caused in the last few human generations, the modern era, the time of the humans: the Anthropocene.

## The Anthropocene

If you have seen the movie Jurassic Park, you may know that the Jurassic is not a type of dinosaur, but instead, a period (201-145

# A Sustainable Life Philosophy

million years ago) in which dinosaurs roamed the Earth.

The people who make up names like Jurassic are geologists who study stratigraphy: the relationship between rock layers and past time. The name given to the 12,000 years since the end of the last Ice Age is the Holocene Epoch. This is a time with a stable climate in which human civilization developed and grew.

In 2016, stratigraphers gathered in South Africa to debate an idea that humans had so changed the world that we were no longer in Holocene-like conditions. It was claimed that we had entered a new geological epoch called the Anthropocene: the Age of the Humans.

However, after nearly a decade of debate, the official ruling came through in March 2024: the Anthropocene does not exist as a geological Epoch, we are still in the Holocene.

# Vita Sapien

Whilst the geologists are arguing over the nitty-gritty of rock science, the rest of society who knows about these things were having a field-day with the concept of the Anthropocene: *the Age of the Humans*.

Some believe that the Age of Humans began 12,000 years ago with the advent of agriculture. Others hold that the Anthropocene began when Columbus brought guns, germs and steel to South America. Others hold that the carbon pollution of the industrial revolution is the beginning of the Anthropocene. The original proposal from the geologists held that the Anthropocene began in the mid-1950s, as evidenced by the radioactive fallout of nuclear bomb tests.

Vita Sapien Philosophy holds that the Anthropocene began with the detonation of the first nuclear bomb – the Alamogordo Test – in New Mexico, USA, on 16 July 1945 at 5.29am Mountain War Time.

## A Sustainable Life Philosophy

This moment in time also serves as the beginning of the Vitan Calendar and is thus the date and time of the Vita New Year celebration, referred to as Earth New Year, a night of Fire and Wine.

The Anthropocene is a fundamental concept for Vita Sapien Philosophy. The name Anthropocene Crisis refers to the multiple, interconnected crises of the modern era including climate change, ecological collapse, nuclear weapons, plastic contamination, global inequality, late-stage capitalism, AI, etc.

A big concern of the Anthropocene Crisis is that human activities are damaging key Earth Systems that are necessary to maintain a safe operating space for humanity. We are breaking through the Planetary Boundaries.

## Planetary Boundaries

Scientists have identified key Earth systems that determine whether Planet Earth remains a good home for humans. Think of these as the warning lights on a planetary dashboard.

There are nine key Earth systems, and the safe boundaries of seven (**bold**) have already been crossed because of human activities:

- The amount of atmospheric CO2 and the energy imbalance of the atmosphere **(Climate Change)**

- Things humans created and released into the environment that nature doesn't know how to deal with **(Novel Entities)**

- Ozone in the upper atmosphere (Stratospheric Ozone Depletion)

- The concentration of particles in the atmosphere that block sunlight (Atmospheric Aerosol Loading)

## A Sustainable Life Philosophy

- The acidity of the ocean (**Ocean Acidification**)

- The amount of nitrogen & phosphorus in the ocean **(Biogeochemical Flows)**

- The amount of freshwater used by humans at the expense of ecosystems **(Freshwater Change)**

- The abundance of forest cover around the world **(Land System Change)**

- The genetic and functional wellbeing of the biosphere **(Biosphere Integrity)**

Vita Sapien Philosophy holds that the primary cause of the Anthropocene Crisis – and breaking through the Planetary Boundaries –

is that people are disconnected from nature, spiritually, emotionally, and intellectually.

An enlightened civilization would never allow Planetary Boundaries to be crossed, in the first place. *Why would they risk it?*

Thus, a solution to the Anthropocene Crisis requires widespread spiritual renaturing—reconnecting people with the Living Planet—which naturally motivates the actions necessary to restore the Planetary Boundaries and return our biosphere to full health.

# The Long Future

Planet Earth is suited to life because our planet's temperature makes it possible for water to exist in all three phases – ice, liquid water, and atmospheric vapour. The temperature is right on Earth because the planet's orbit is neither too close, nor too far from the Sun, and because nature has mechanisms for regulating greenhouse gases for temperature control (Gaia Theory).

# A Sustainable Life Philosophy

Earth's orbit is said to lie within the Habitable Zone–the Goldilocks Zone–and will do so for another two billion years or more.

Beyond this time, the Sun will massively expand into a Red Giant as it ages and consumes its fuel. Eventually Earth will be baked dry and lifeless.

*Earth orbits within the Habitable Zone of the Sun.*

Vita Sapien Philosophy refers to the remaining 2 billion years in which life can exist on Earth as the Long Future. While some forms of life may persist for two billion years—e.g. bacteria living in rocks kilometres below the seafloor—humans will be long gone.

A potential future state in the early portion of the Long Future is the Verdant Age, the time when humans and the Living Planet thrive in synergy.

The Verdant Age is Vita Sapien Philosophy's North Star and is discussed in detail later.

Standing in the way of achieving the Verdant Age is the dire state of Planet Earth which is presently on trajectory to be becoming worse than the condition of the biosphere during the Permian Extinction.

## Worse than the Permian

The Permian Extinction—the Great Dying— 253 million years ago is a frame of reference for our present predicament.

Massive volcanic eruptions in the Siberian Traps began around 300,000 years before the extinction event. For hundreds of thousands of years, Earth's carbon sinks absorbed these volcanic emissions. However, when magma intrusions reached vast coal deposits buried in the crust, everything changed.

# A Sustainable Life Philosophy

The coal combustion released enormous additional volumes of $CO_2$, methane, and toxic gases—a carbon bomb that overwhelmed the planet's ability to cope. Over approximately 30,000 to 60,000 years, the $CO_2$ raised global temperatures about 10 degrees Celsius, warming and acidifying the ocean. The warm ocean became stratified, meaning oxygen-rich surface waters failed to mix with waters below, starving the deeper ocean of life.

Around 90% of marine species and 70% of terrestrial species went extinct, nearly ending complex life on Earth. Volcanism continued for another half-million years after the extinction. It took 10-20 million years for life to evolve a comparable level of biodiversity.

Now consider that humans have set in motion a planetary catastrophe that is potentially worse than the Permian Extinction for three reasons.

First, we are similarly pumping massive amounts of $CO_2$ into the atmosphere—over 2 trillion tons to date. However, rather than doing this over 30,000+ years, we are releasing $CO_2$ approximately 10 times faster than during the deadly phase of the Permian extinction. We've accomplished this catastrophic release in just 300 years since the Industrial Revolution began.

Today, carbon sinks are failing, and natural positive-feedback processes are kicking in, driving temperatures higher and out of our control. We have not even started to reduce emissions, let alone end them.

Second, most of the 9 billion tons of plastics we have manufactured reside in landfills that were not designed for the massive superstorms that are coming. These monster storms could scour-out the world's landfills and flush the contents into the ocean.

# A Sustainable Life Philosophy

The Coelacanth is an ancient type of fish that survived the Permian Extinction and exists today living in caves hundreds of meters below the sea surface.

A Coelacanth was found dead in Indonesian waters, having choked on a Lay's potato chip packet.

It is chilling to think that a species that survived the Great Dying might be susceptible to extinction from something as ubiquitous as chip packets floating in the sea.

For the chip packets and other bits of plastic that don't get eaten by wildlife, there is another path: weathering. This is the process where the plastic degrades into smaller and smaller pieces due to sunlight and physical action. Macro plastics become microplastics become nanoplastics and these are now widespread across the entire biosphere from the clouds to the oceans to the internal organs of humans and many other creatures. We have saturated the biosphere in plastic particles that are contaminated with dyes, flame retardants and softening agents.

This is the nature of the Anthropocene—we've created threats that evolution never prepared life on Earth to face.

Third, potential ionising radiation from nuclear war and nuclear power station meltdown.

Today, there are around 12,000 nuclear weapons dotted around the world with most being held by the USA and Russia, many of which are located in forward operating bases and could be deployed at short notice.

Besides nuclear weapons, there are 450 or so nuclear power stations hundreds of thousands of tons of highly radioactive spent fuel that needs generations of maintenance to remain safe. There is a huge risk of ionising radiation escaping into the biosphere if the human technocratic system fails to maintain them.

# A Sustainable Life Philosophy

The speed of the carbon emissions, the plastics, and the threat of ionising radiation from nukes all point to the potential for a profound mass-extinction event, with us humans among the first tranche of organisms to go. We risk setting back Earth's evolutionary clock hundreds of millions of years.

This is why we need a spiritual transformation to reconnect people to our global ecosystem and transform our relationship to the Living Planet while we still have time. But we are running out of time.

The 2025 paper *Planetary Solvency – Finding Our Balance with Nature* describes a worst-case scenario in which climate collapse kills off half of humanity by 2050—just 25 years from the time of writing. This is alarming, yes. But is it alarmist? No.

The *Planetary Solvency* paper came from the University of Exeter and was written by actuaries—the professionals who calculate risk for the insurance industry.

If there is only a 1% chance of this catastrophe being true we should pursue the solution with all the vigour we can muster.

Like it or not, collapse is upon us. We have simply done too much damage to the planet and have too momentum for us to avoid things getting worse before they get better.

We are going into collapse; it's already begun. But collapse needn't be fatal. It could be survivable. But to survive we need a Full Transition away from our unsustainable global system and toward an alternative, ecologically sustainable civilization.

As we are already over 1.2°C above the pre-industrial baseline, we are well within the Hothouse Danger Zone as described in the *Trajectories* paper.

The diagram from the *Trajectories* paper has been adapted for simplicity, showing two

# A Sustainable Life Philosophy

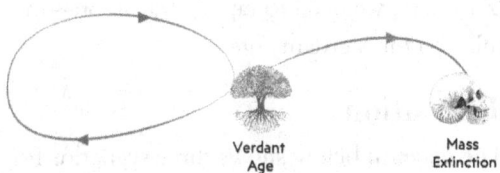

Verdant Age

Mass Extinction

potential futures: the Verdant Age or Mass Extinction.

Mass Extinction is represented by the Anthronaut symbol, comprised of a nautilus shell and a human skull. The human skull is symbolic of the extinction of the human race. The nautilus shell reminds us that it is possible for species to survive hundreds of millions of years.

The nautilus itself has remained largely unchanged for over 500 million years, having survived all the mass extinction events, even the Permian.

Today, the nautilus is vulnerable to extinction as they are being remorselessly poached. If we are to protect the nautilus and the rest of the biosphere, we need to rapidly transition—in full—to the Verdant Age.

## Transition

The diagram below shows three scenarios for transition:

- Full Transition
- Partial Transition
- Zero Transition.

The concentric circles in the diagram show the depth of collapse associated with the three levels of transition.

- **Full Transition**: the outer ring representing a shallow collapse that humanity can survive

- **Partial Transition**: the middle ring shows collapse so deep that human survival remains in doubt even after

## A Sustainable Life Philosophy

the collapse has resolved

- **No Transition**: the inner ring shows collapse that is so deep it leads to mass extinction including human extinction.

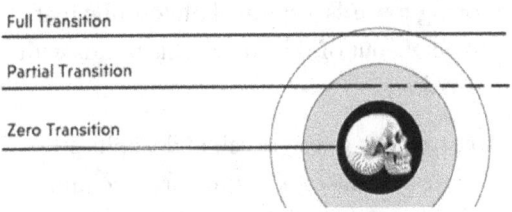

Three degrees of transition: Full, Partial, Zero.

Achieving Full Transition to the Verdant Age is a herculean task and it probably can't be achieved with the present widespread state of spiritual disconnection to nature.

For Full Transition, we need a global Spiritual Renaturing. What might that look like? For some it might start with a belief in Gya.

***Note***: *the Stockdale Paradox calls us to stare in to the abyss. We have done that. If you feel overwhelmed or emotional, that's because you have been paying attention. Thank you. Now we can begin building a new future, the Verdant Age.*

Now that we have a clear understanding of our situation grounded in science, let us start moving towards a spiritual philosophy that can get us out of this mess. This begins with a cosmology.

A cosmology is a spiritual/philosophical overview of the origin, structure, evolution, and ultimate fate of the world.

# Vita Sapien Cosmology

Vita Sapien Cosmology is here described in eleven waypoints along a timeline from the beginning of the Universe to the end of life on Earth, a billion year or so from now.

# A Sustainable Life Philosophy

- **Big Bang:** about 13.8 billion years ago, this is the earliest point we can observe and measure with current physics—but not necessarily the absolute beginning of existence.

- **Sun and Earth**: About 4.6 billion years ago, the solar nebula—a giant molecular cloud — gravitationally collapses, with most mass collecting in the centre to form the Sun while the rest flattened into a protoplanetary disk where Earth and the other planets formed.

- **Bioprima:** the origination of life on Earth arising from non-living chemical compounds, also called abiogenesis.

- **Gyagenesis**: The Cambrian Explosion, approximately 540 million years ago, when most major animal body plans emerged and complex ecological relationships formed, marking the birth of Gya as an interconnected, self-regulating biosphere.

— **Genus Homo:** the evolution of Homo erectus about 2 million years ago as the first of the human family to spread across continents.

— **Primasapien:** the emergence of modern Homo sapien cognition when engineering, art and spirituality converged as powerful forces shaping human culture, a complex, timely evolution that is centred around 70,000 years ago.

— **Axial Age:** approximately 800-200 BCE, the emergence of new spiritual and religious beliefs across Eurasia, leading significant human societies to sever their natural spiritual bond to nature in exchange for otherworldly spiritualities.

# A Sustainable Life Philosophy

— **Anthropocene:** The age in which humans become the main drivers of planetary change in the climate and environment. Vita Sapien marks the beginning of this age with the Alamogordo atomic bomb test—the first nuclear explosion—on July 16, 1945. This is the beginning of the Vita Sapien calender.

— **Verdant Age:** Potentially beginning sometime with the coming decades, a mass movement triggers Homo sapiens to awake spiritually to the Living Planet and begin the transition to an ecologically sustainable civilization that thrives in synergy with the biosphere for a Galactic Year, about 230 million Earth years.

— **Sapiofinalis:** more than 230 million years in the future, the last humans on Earth as major planetary forces including solar brightening, atmospheric oxygen

depletion, and the moist greenhouse transition render Earth uninhabitable for complex life.
- **Gyafinalis**: 800 million to 1 billion years from now, when rising solar luminosity causes the collapse of complex ecosystems and the death of Gya as a living, interconnected biosphere. Thereafter, Biofinalis, as the last living organisms perish.

Today, we are in Anthropocene, and if we can survive the 21$^{st}$ Century, it is possible we can enter the Verdant Age. This is much more likely to happen if the dominant spirituality is ecologically sustainable. Ecosystem Spirituality is framed specifically to survive the Anthropocene and advance the Verdant Age.

A Sustainable Life Philosophy

# Ecosystem Spirituality

Ecosystem Spirituality distinguishes Vita Sapien spiritual view from other similar frames such as ecospirituality, spiritual ecology or ecological spirituality. These are nature-spiritual beliefs that are infused Christian theology or New Age thinking, particularly eco-versions of Buddhism. There is merit in all of them, however Ecosystem Spirituality is specifically framed to Advance the Verdant Age.

There are four sections in this chapter.

## Vita Sapien

- **Gya** describes a the Living Planet through a spiritual lens.

- **Four Dimensions** frames Ecosystem Spirituality across time and space, creating the context of the idea.

- **Eight Themes** help people understand the subject of spirituality which makes it easier to understand how spirituality exists in our lives.

- **Experience & Practice** examines how nature influences us spiritually and how we can engage in spiritual practice with nature.

# Gya

In Earth system science is Gaia Theory which postulates that life on Earth behaves in the manner of a single organism. This is because life on Earth modifies the composition of the

# A Sustainable Life Philosophy

atmosphere and ocean to maintain chemical and thermal equilibrium that is conducive to an abundance of life.

Life begets life.

When Gaia Theory was first published in 1974 – back then referred to as the *Gaia Hypothesis* – it helped trigger the environmental movement with the call: 'The Earth is Alive'.

Vita Sapien Philosophy accepts this science and uses it as the foundation of a spiritual belief called *Gya*.

Note: the words Gaia and Gya are pronounced the same despite different spelling.

- Gaia is a scientific theory that life on Earth behaves in the manner of a living organism.

## Vita Sapien

— Gya is a spiritual belief that life on Earth is a living organism.

Unlike Gaia, which is a scientific theory, Gya is a spiritual belief. When people believe in Gya they see themselves as part of a planetary life-force.

You don't have to believe in Gya to follow Vita Sapien Philosophy. It's a spiritual option.

However, when you do believe in Gya, you are more likely to identify yourself <u>as a part of</u> the Living Planet. The alternative is to see yourself <u>as apart from</u> the Living Planet, which is the normal view in the West.

When you see yourself as a part of the Living Planet, you understand that there is no 'away' to throw things to, and polluting the environment is akin to polluting yourself.

Landfills are not just municipal waste disposal facilities; they are wounds in the body of Gya.

# A Sustainable Life Philosophy

When you see yourself as a part of the Living Planet, you understand that your well-being is intertwined. If the planet dies, we all die with her.

To help flesh-out the idea of Gya, here are some of her characteristics:

- **He, She, or It?** – Technically, Gya would be referred to as an 'it' as it is a gender-less, non-human species. However, out of reverence Gya is referred to as 'she'.

- **Grown, Not Created, Not God** – Gya is neither a God, a deity, nor the creator of the universe. Instead, Gya is an emergent property of the laws of nature – in particular biology, physics, and chemistry – playing out on Planet Earth. Gya arose spontaneously, around 3.8 billion years ago, when conditions allowed.

## Vita Sapien

- **Not Conscious** – Gya does not have consciousness, intent, or free will except to the extent that humans confer it to her. Humans are the part of nature that has free will.

- **Wide & Thin** – Gya has the shape of a thin-walled sphere, with the wall thickness about 0.5% of the diameter of the sphere. Think of Earth as a ping-pong ball full of rock. The skin of the ping-pong ball is analogous to the relative diameter of Gya.

- **Above & Below** – Above Gya is the frigid depth of space, and below Gya is the Earth's mantle and molten rock. Gya's wispy outer boundary is about 100 kilometres above the ground. Her lower boundary is some kilometres below the seafloor in the

## A Sustainable Life Philosophy

Earth's crust where microscopic organisms are known to live in the pores of rocks.

- **Very Old** – Gya has endured about 3.8 billion years because she maintains internal chemical and thermal equilibrium that is conducive to life. If the Universe is 13.8 billion years old, that makes Gya about one-quarter the age of the Universe.

- **Not judging** – Gya is not conscious, and she doesn't judge us for our actions. However, she does respond to them at the global scale. If we continue to pump 50 billion tons of heat trapping $CO_2$ gas into the atmosphere every year, we can expect a dramatic reaction.

## Vita Sapien

- **We are welcome here** – Humans came to be a part of Gya through the same evolutionary process as the trees and the bees, the whales, and the snails. We are as welcome on this planet as they are.

- **Habitable for Humans** – Over the past 3.8 billion years, Gya has existed in many forms not all of which were suited to human habitation. At times in the past, it has been neither too hot nor too cold on Earth for humans.

- **Gya's climate** has been ideal for the growth of human civilization over the past few million years. However, our actions are shifting Gya into a new climactic phase that will be hostile to human life.

# A Sustainable Life Philosophy

- **Many names** – there are many names that describe ideas similar to Gya. The term Living Planet is used throughout this book and can be taken as being broadly synonymous to biosphere, Gaia and Gya. Similar words also include *Gaea* the Ancient Greek Goddess of Earth and the source of the name Gaia. There is also Mother Nature, Pachamama, and many other names from different cultures.

- **A Species** – If Gya is a living organism then she needs a proper scientific name. It is proposed that Gya be given the name: *Imperium vitae-planeta*, which roughly translates from Latin to Empire of the Living Planet. *Vitae-planeta* is a unique species in that it is a single individual comprised of a complex interconnected web of all life on Earth.

- **Spiritual Belief** – Gya is not a scientifically validated idea, although it is very close to the concept of Gaia Theory.

This is a really important point. You see, science and spirituality are natural partners as they both help us understand the world around us, and to establish our right relation to that reality.

It was established in the opening pages of this book that the Cognitive Revolution opened a reservoir of both rational and spiritual thinking in humans.

In the German language, the word 'gheist' has a broad meaning encompassing both intellect and spirituality. Similarly, Vita Sapien Philosophy sees spirituality and scientific enquiry stemming from the same source.

# A Sustainable Life Philosophy

Cognition relates to intellectual and spiritual wisdom.

Belief in Gya—or respect for Gaia Theory—expresses itself through what Vita Sapien Philosophy calls **Ecosystem Spirituality**—a four-dimensional framework for understanding our bond with the Living Planet.

# Four Dimensions

Ecosystem Spirituality is specific, scientific, and a response to the Anthropocene Crisis—spirituality with purpose: to maintain the conditions that allow life to thrive on Earth.

Ecosystem Spirituality refers to a human having a foundational spiritual bond with life on Earth.

There are four dimensions that outline the spatial, temporal and contextual frame of the spiritual belief: **Scale, Time, Scope and Depth**

## Scale

Ecosystem Spirituality describes spiritual relationships with life across dimensions of distance and size:

- **Microbial scale:** The microbiome ecosystem within us—the bacteria, fungi, and other organisms that make up around 60% of our cells.

- **Local ecosystems:** Your aquarium, backyard, walking path, or daily environment.

- **Bioregional:** Place-based spirituality that connects people to a specific landscape, as seen in many Indigenous worldviews.

- **Planetary:** The global ecosystem, encompassing concerns such as climate change, ocean acidification, and the Planetary Boundaries.

# A Sustainable Life Philosophy

- **Trans-planetary** considers the influence of factors beyond Earth on the biosphere, such as the Sun, Moon and Earth-impacting asteroids

## Time

Ecosystem Spirituality unfolds across time:

- **Deep Past:** Contemplation of bioprima—the origins of life on Earth—and billions of years of evolutionary process.

- **The Present:** Immediate connection with life on Earth here and now. What's happening to the biosphere on the evening news.

- **Near Future:** Humanity's transition to a sustainable civilization over and beyond the 21st Century.

- **The Long Future:** Maintaining ecosystem integrity for a *Galactic Year*

—230 million Earth years into the future.

## Scope

Scope considers the human systems that interact with the Living Planet:

- **Technology:** From Stone Age archery to thermonuclear weapons—technology beneficial, neutral and harmful impacts on the Living Planet.

- **Infrastructure:** including energy, transportation, agriculture, and urban systems.

- **Economy:** a powerful driver of human behaviour includes capitalism, the ecology of commerce, circular economy, and degrowth approaches.

- **Politics:** governance, policy, and power structures—from local to geopolitics.

# A Sustainable Life Philosophy

- **Belief Systems:** religion, philosophy, and worldview. Understanding how belief systems—such as Armageddon—shapes the world.

Ecosystem Spirituality recognises that protecting nature means understanding and engaging with these systems, not escaping or denying them.

## Depth

Depth situates Ecosystem Spirituality within a matrix of cognitive capabilities—intellectual, emotional, and sensory—enabling rich interactions with ecosystems.

Depth transforms ecological awareness into:

- **Lived Experience:** a direct, embodied connection with nature.

- **Meaningful Engagement:** Finding personal purpose through a personal relationship with life on Earth.

- **Pro-Ecosystem Intent:** a motivation to live sustainably and support life to thrive.

Deep engagement means feeling grief when forests burn, joy when species recover, and purpose when dedicating one's life to ecological restoration and advancing the Verdant Age.

Understanding how Ecosystem Spirituality can be a part of your life requires a deeper understanding of the subject of spirituality as described in the Eight Themes.

# Eight Themes

Ecosystem Spirituality becomes easy to understand when there is a common vocabulary that describes *the subject* of spirituality, as opposed to just the lived experience.

# A Sustainable Life Philosophy

Its the difference between liking a popular painting and understanding what it is about the painting that is likeable.

Vita Sapien Philosophy views the term 'spirituality' as an umbrella concept that shelters many themes. Eight themes are listed below, with multiple subthemes.

Vita Sapien Philosophy does not claim that these themes represent the totality of spiritual experience. Instead, they form a simple frame of reference to make it easy to talk about the subject of spirituality.

In this way, we are better able to discuss the potential for spirituality to foster radical pro-environmental behaviour change.

Ecosystem Spirituality does't sit in opposition to other spiritual beliefs, but is co-operative, encouraging people to care about the Living Planet irrespective of belief.

## Vita Sapien

Anyone with the three core traits—a spiritual bond to nature, trust in science, and commitment to action—can be considered a Vitan.

Thus there can be Vitan Christians, Vitan Atheists, Vitan Hindus, Vitan Buddhists, and so on. Ecosystem Spirituality can augment existing beliefs with ecological consciousness rather than demanding their abandonment.

People of faith may find contradictory views in Ecosystem Spirituality, particularly around the scientific understanding of the origins of life on Earth. There is nothing wrong with this as humans are able to comfortably hold conflicting ideas.

The Eight Themes are listed below, beginning with *The Bigger Thing*.

# A Sustainable Life Philosophy

**1.    The Bigger Thing**

**2.    The Golden Rule**

**3.    Life's Big Questions**
Where did we come from—Why are we here—What happens when we die?

**4.    Journey Within**
Inner Self—Grounding—Self-Actualisation

**5.    Transcendence**
Peak & Trough Experience—Awe, Wonder & Amazement—Timelessness & Flow

**6.    Deep Feelings**
Phenomena & Insight—Sacred & Profane—*Raison d'etre*

**7.    Good & Evil**

**8.    Spirit & Soul**

Vita Sapien

# The Bigger Thing

One of the most common concepts that describes spirituality is an individual's quest to identify as part of something bigger than themselves.

For some people the Bigger Thing is God, and for others, say professional athletes, it is their sport.

People's behaviour is guided in part by their efforts to contribute to the success or advancement of the Bigger Thing. Furthermore, people can be part of multiple Bigger Things.

To advance the Verdant Age, we should see ourselves as a part of the biosphere, with Gaia or Gya. As with the trees and bees, the whales and snails, we humans are cells in the body of the Living Planet.

Holding this belief profoundly changes our relationship to the environment, as we see that the environment is us: an interconnected, holistic 'oneness'. An interbeing.

When you identify with the biosphere and the social movement to protect her, you are advancing your own life support system. So, this is not only spiritually rewarding, but wholly logical, as well.

## The Golden Rule

A Golden Rule is a central, guiding statement that frames ethical and rational decision making. The world's major religions all share a common Golden Rule which goes something like this: *Do unto others as you would have them do unto you.*

The problem with this 'Do unto others' statement is that it fails to take into consideration the Living Planet that is our life support system.

As discussed, during the Axial Age when the major religions were formed, there was no imminent threat to the natural world.

Vita Sapien's Golden Rule is thus:

> Do unto others <u>and the Living Planet</u> as you would have them do unto you.

Phrased another way:

> Be good to people and the Living Planet, and they will be good to you.

# Life's Big Questions

Spirituality offers answers to imponderable questions, but three are particularly important.

- Where did we come from?
- Why are we here?
- What happens when we die?

**Where did we come from?**
*What are the origins of the human race?*

To answer this Big Question we ought to speak to cosmologists and biologists because these questions can be answered by science and our understanding gets better year by year.

# A Sustainable Life Philosophy

The best science to date suggests that the Universe formed around 13.8 billion years ago with a rapid expansion called the Big Bang. The Sun and Earth formed around 4.5 billions years ago.

The first living things on Earth formed from non-living substrates compounds around 3.8 billion years ago. From this bioprima event, behaviourally modern humans arose through a long process of evolution around 70,000 years ago.

We humans and the other living things alive today are the survivors of five Mass Extinction Events. We are made of what Earth is made of. We grew here with the trees and the bees, the whales, and the snails. We belong here. This is our planet that we share with an abundance of other living beings.

## Why Are We Here?
*What is the purpose of human existence?*

# Vita Sapien

Vita Sapien Philosophy holds that humans are here on Earth for the same reason as the trees, the bees, the whales, and the snails: to pursue our individual life interests in a manner that makes a positive contribution to the whole.

In this case, the whole is human society and the Living Planet, both of which are our collective life support system.

That's why we are here.

I am going to repeat that because it is such an important point:

The purpose of human existence is to pursue our personal interests in a manner that benefits the well-being of the whole.

## What Happens When We Die?
*What happens to us upon death?*

Vita Sapien Philosophy holds that when the body dies, the person dies with it. However, the material and energy in our body enters the biophysical flux and may be *revitalised* by being taken up by other organisms. In this way, the end of our life begets the beginning of new life.

# Journey Within

The Journey Within consists of three key aspects:

- Inner Self
- Grounding
- Self-Actualisation

# Inner Self

The Inner Self represents the unique essence of every individual human being–an aspect of being that can be explored through personal introspection, often in solitude and quiet contemplation.

The Inner Self is not isolated but exists in relationship to all of life. Understanding that we are part of a greater web of life – connected to nature, other beings, and the

Earth – deepens our sense of purpose and enhances our spiritual journey.

People can find deeper insights into their Inner Self through meditation, yoga and other spiritual avenues. This is good. We ought to understand ourselves at this deep level, it leads to a more fulfilling life.

However, here is the problem. Most of what falls under the umbrella of spirituality in the Western World is basically just self-help. Yoga makes you feel good. Meditation makes you feel better. This is good.

But it's not just us that needs help. The biosphere needs help. The biosphere needs a ton of help if it is to remain in a form that sustains human life on Earth.

Ecosystem Spirituality helps foster spiritual practice that allows us to protect the biological life-support system on Earth. Investigate your Inner Self to find the power to change the outer world.

A Sustainable Life Philosophy

# Grounding

Grounding is the recognition of our place within the interconnected whole. It is knowing where home is, where we belong, and how we fit within the vastness of human society, the biosphere, and time itself – past and future.

New Age spirituality tells us that the atoms in our bodies were forged inside stars, that we are made of Star Dust, and to believe in the Cosmos as you are a child of the Universe.

There are grains of truth here, but a more relevant framing is that <u>we are children of the biosphere</u>. That's the grounding we need to survive the 21$^{st}$ Century and thrive beyond.

The visible universe is 96 billion light years in diameter and there are cosmological phenomena that have a bearing on life on Earth including cosmic radiation, asteroids, coronal mass ejections, and so on. However, these are beyond our circle of control and of far lesser immediate concern than the atmospheric concentration of $CO_2$ and the well-being of forests and phytoplankton.

New Age Spirituality has engaged millions in spiritual inquiry, but often without grounding in environmental science or pragmatic, physical reality.

When people hold the living systems that sustain us—forests, oceans, plankton—as sacred with the same intensity they reserve for cosmic mysteries or crystals, we will have turned a corner toward the Verdant Age.

# Self-Actualisation

Self-Actualisation is the pursuit of one's highest potential – living authentically in alignment with one's values and purpose.

- **Self-Reflection** – Examining thoughts, emotions, and beliefs to cultivate self–awareness

# A Sustainable Life Philosophy

- **Expediency** – Continuously refining one's skills, influence, and effectiveness over time

Self-actualisation is important if we are to be effective agents for change to advance the Verdant Age. Be the best you can be for life on Earth.

## Transcendence

Transcendence refers to those times when you feel yourself to go beyond the normal experience of life. Three sub-themes are identified:

- Peak & Trough Experience
- Awe, Wonder & Amazement
- Timelessness & Flow

While these sub-themes are given distinct names, they are often experienced overlapping with one another.

# Peak & Trough Experience

Peak & Trough experience refers to intense pleasurable or painful experiences that powerfully shape us. They can often be sensed during the same situation—think of a roller-coaster ride, both exhilarating and terrifying in equal measure. Extreme experience—whether perceived as good or bad—opens a doorway to spiritual change, and therefore, potentially to the adoption of nature spirituality.

**Peak Experience**

Peak Experience refers to those moments of euphoria and bliss when you are detached from your normal reality and become enthralled and entranced by an uplifting experience. A pathway to a fulfilling life is to regularly enjoy peak experiences.

Ecosystem Spirituality holds that when we enjoy peak experience through nature, we more closely bond with Gya, the Living Planet, our life support system.

# A Sustainable Life Philosophy

**Trough Experience**

Trough Experience refers to those instances where you are flattened, rendered helpless, approaching what feels like death. This can be brought about through near-death experience, witnessing a tragic accident, war, physical assault, attack by wild animals, etc. Trough experience is not pleasant, but it can trigger a substantial shift in our spirituality.

Getting dumped by a big wave very quickly shifts your perceived relationship to the ocean.

Many environmental activists have trough experience through being beaten or jailed for standing up for the planet, but this serves to strengthen their resolve.

## Awe, Wonder & Amazement

The words awe, wonder and amazement refer to the instances when we feel overwhelmed or taken aback by the vastness or extraordinariness of an experience. Such experiences are often associated with *Aesthetic Chills* where an experience triggers powerful and lasting emotional feeling that can result a person rethinking their values and worldview.

People can find awe and wonderment in many different places including from such obscure sources such as drag races or watching YouTube videos of rocket launches, or the manufacturing process of golf balls.

Ecosystem Spirituality calls us to seek awe, wonder and amazement in natural landscapes and the social movements such as the growing rebellion against extinction.

## Timelessness & Flow

Timelessness comes when circumstances are so distracting that one loses track of the passage of time. Flow is where one is engaged in effortless action with total focus.

One could fall experience timelessness and flow watching your underwear in a tumble dryer or sitting under a metal triangle chanting

# A Sustainable Life Philosophy

'*Ohmmm*' but these won't point your spiritual compass towards the Living Planet.

Ecosystem Spirituality teaches that we should seek timelessness and flow in nature: a waterfall, a walk on a beach, kayaking across a lake, the sights and sounds of life on Earth.

Get into flow by reading books or articles about the Earth System. Lose track of time in the garden or a forest or in conversations about how to advance the Verdant Age.

## Deep Feelings

These are the feelings that strongly held, and for which one will make sacrifices to defend.

- Phenomena & Insight
- Sacred & Profane
- *Raison d'etre*

### Phenomena & Insight

One aspect of spirituality lies in how we interpret experiences and emotions that lack clear, rational explanation. Some people approach these phenomena through a scientific lens, while others perceive a deeper, mystical dimension.

Some people, for example, claim to have extra-sensory perception, or to have communicated with people who have died, beings of other dimensions, or a god.

Take UFOs, for example. Seeing an unfamiliar pattern of lights in the night sky, one person might assume they are witnessing an alien spacecraft, while another might simply acknowledge that the airspace is busy and accept that not everything is immediately explainable.

Many who believe in UFOs subscribe to the idea of a hidden reality—an unseen realm operating alongside everyday existence. This perspective extends to beliefs in crystals, tarot, and other phenomena associated with New Age spirituality. At times, people experience an overwhelming sense that they must follow a particular course of action, holding to this

# A Sustainable Life Philosophy

conviction as strongly as if they had material proof.

There is much in the universe that remains unexplained, and space for mystery and wonder is part of a rich spiritual life. The question isn't whether these experiences are 'real'—but whether they help or hinder our ability to respond to the climate and ecological crisis.

If your spiritual explorations lead you toward nature reverence and ecological action, they serve the Verdant Age.

If they become an escape from reality, they may be working against it. The biosphere is in crisis. While we can hold space for mystery, our primary spiritual and intellectual focus must be on understanding and protecting the Earth systems that sustain all life.

Learn how forests create rain. Understand ocean currents and carbon cycles. Marvel at the complexity of soil ecosystems.

# Vita Sapien

The Living Planet and the Earth System itself is the greatest mystery worth exploring.

## Sacred & Profane

The sacred are those things that are perceived to be imbued with unique and higher qualities and values, and for which distinct rules apply. Profane is simply something that lacks sacredness, such as the everyday and mundane. Sacredness is not implicit but is granted by one's beliefs.

Ecosystem Spirituality holds that we can choose what we believe to be sacred and if we are to advance the Verdant Age, the following need to be seen as sacred:

- Places of ecological significance are sacred as are acts of personal sacrifice on behalf of the biosphere

- Natural biophysical processes that underpin our life support system are sacred, and we should act accordingly

# A Sustainable Life Philosophy

   by protecting them

- Indigenous cultures and endangered species are sacred and ought to be revered and protected

Sacred & Profane also builds on the basic principle of right and wrong which signifies actions that either help or hinder achieving a desired state. A desirable state for human civilization is a healthy biosphere populated by healthy, happy people for millions of years into the future.

Vita Sapien Philosophy holds that harming people and the biosphere is wrong, and actions that help people and Advance the Verdant Age are right. Of equal importance, inaction in the face of wrongdoing is itself wrong.

Those who hold power, wealth, or influence and deploy it against the well-being of people and life on Earth—whether through fossil fuel extraction, ecosystem destruction, or blocking climate action—are agents of harm that must be opposed.

While individuals have agency and can choose differently, our opposition must be predominantly focused on dismantling the systems that enable and reward planetary destruction. Both matter: destructive systems create perverse incentives, while individuals with power make choices that perpetuate or challenge those systems.

## Raison d'etre

*Raison d'etre* is a French term meaning reason to be—the meaning of an individual's life.

Some people attach themselves to a cause so tightly that they experience *Identity Fusion*, a visceral sense of oneness with their belief. Identity Fusion can be a positive or negative for the Living Planet. For example, activists in the rebellion against extinction fuse their identity with a cause that advances the Verdant Age.

Vita Sapien Philosophy holds that the Anthropocene Crisis calls upon us to set our *raison d'etre* to the highest levels of Earthwork: Advancing the Verdant Age.

Your *raison d'etre* will determine what rituals and ceremonies are meaningful to you. Your *raison d'etre* will determine the causes you support and those people who you regard as significant others, leaders and heroes.

If you are to fuse your identity, fuse it with the integrity of the biosphere and the proper function of the Earth System as these are fundamental to life on Earth and for human civilization to prosper.

## Good & Evil

In contemporary use, the word evil has religious overtones. However, the Old English root word *yfel* refers to exceeding limits and causing harm. Ecosystem Spirituality applies this ancient meaning to actions and systems that harm the biosphere and transgress planetary limits.

**Structural Evil** relates to actions that exceed Planetary Boundaries and cause extensive biospheric harm. The evil exists in the harm itself, magnified by culpability. **Wilfully Ignorant Evil** occurs when individuals fail to investigate harm despite having the duty and resources to do so—think fossil fuel executives who never take the time to study climate science. **Full Knowing Evil** occurs when individuals knowingly perpetrate harm despite awareness of the consequences—think forestry corporation executives approving logging in the full knowledge that it risks the extinction of the koala.

The emerging international legislative framework around ecocide provides legal grounding for evil. It is the duty of Vitans (and others) to oppose evil—to dismantle systems that exceed planetary boundaries, to prevent those who perpetrate ecocide from continuing their destruction, and to ensure they are prosecuted under emerging ecocide (or other) laws to the fullest extent.

The fossil fuel industry represents structural evil that is, for now, a *necessary evil*—required to maintain agriculture and economic function during the transition. However, necessity does not negate its evilness. The fossil fuel industry must be deliberately and systematically euthanized, ensuring minimal harm during its planned extinction while urgently building the ecologically sustainable energy systems that will replace it.

## Spirit & Soul

Ecosystem Spirituality doesn't teach belief in gods or an everlasting soul. What matters is our relationship with the Living Planet, which can be understood through three types of spirit:

## Vita Sapien

- **Somatic Spirit** is the animating essence of a living being characterised by movement, growth, breath, heartbeat, reproduction, and so on. Humans, animals and plants have a somatic spirit while they are alive, but this dies when they die.

- **Exosomatic Spirit** refers to that which a living being leaves behind. For a human that may be fond memories in the minds of families and friends, or books they wrote. The exosomatic spirit of the Dutch painter van Gough remains dominant over a hundred years after his death. However, the exosomatic spirit of the man who fixed van Gough's shoes is lost in the annals of time. Animals and plants can also have an Exosomatic Spirit. The imprints of fossilised animals, for example, or a painting of a particular tree. The story of Moby Dick is the exosomatic spirit of the author and of a white sperm whale.

- **Parasomatic Spirit** refers to the perception that some inanimate objects are alive. For example, a piece of concrete in the shape of a cat can give the sensation of having met a real living animal. Parasomatic Spirit is analogous to the Kami in Japanese Shinto culture. Kami are spiritual entities believed to reside in waterfalls and groves, and indicated by the presence of the red archway, the *Torii*. Ghosts are an example of a Parasomatic spirit.

This chapter has so far provided a rational explanation of Ecosystem Spirituality. Now, let's consider these ideas from an emotional perspective.

We have done the thinking, now let's do the feeling.

# Experience & Practice

All the above works on the rational mind. Now we need to use words to speak to the heart.

- **Nature Calls** describes ways that we can perceive nature through the spiritual lens.
- **Reaching Out** describes practices we can undertake to get closer to nature, spiritually.

## Nature Calls

Drowning Doesn't Look Like Drowning, remember. We have to be in tune to nature to understand her. To feel her. To change the world, we need to be able to hear nature calling out to us.

Nature is calling out to us all the time. Can you hear her?

# A Sustainable Life Philosophy

*Nature Calls Out* are those instances when nature intervenes into your consciousness. Read each little phrase below, then close your eyes and go there.

How many of these have you sensed, and what would you add to this list?

> *—the wind changes to a cool breeze as the storm approaches*
>
> *—you hear small animals rustling in the grass*
>
> *—the multicoloured glow of a rainbow in a waterfall's mist*
>
> *— the spangles of dappled sunlight through a forest canopy*
>
> *— the unique diversity of colour and texture of lichen on a boulder*
>
> *—a bird lands on a branch close to you, taking you by surprise*
>
> *—you come across a fallen tree covered in fungi and moss as it returns to the soil*

# Vita Sapien

*—you see a bird on a branch with an insect in its beak*

*—a possum climbing up a tree turns to look at you*

*—the Full Moon breaks through the clouds to illuminate the ocean horizon*

*—the sun sets in an orange sky*

*—a dolphin comes to the surface, and you hear its breath*

*—clear sea water washes against green seaweed on the rocks, lolling back and forth*

*—you see the first sign of a new leaf on a pot-plant*

*—a bird lands on your windowsill and looks inside*

Nature is all around us. She is calling out to us. Asking us to care for her. Can you hear her?

It is imperative that you hear her, and care for her. We are going into dark times, and we need all-hands-on deck, emotionally prepared for what is coming down the pipeline.

A Sustainable Life Philosophy

# Reaching Out

When people fill their spirituality with nature this guides them towards right action to Advance the Verdant Age.

Here are some simple practices that help you connect spiritually to nature.

*—Practice Vitan Meditation by losing time looking at or listening to nature. Maybe close your eyes and listen to birdsong, gaze into a fish tank, or listening to a guided Vitan meditation.*

*—Take your shoes off and walk on the ground, on the grass, in the mud, on the beach*

*—When it rains, find somewhere to watch the water fall from the sky. Maybe stand in the rain.*

*—Do a Moonscope to determine when and where the Full Moon rises and then watch it. Experience the Moon Illusion alone or with friends*

## Vita Sapien

*—Stand close to a native animal and just look at it. See if you can encourage the animal to look at you. Maybe you can be friends*

*—Close your eyes for five minutes and then open them to gaze upon an old leaf*

*—Watch a documentary about nature, concentrate on learning the new information, then ponder it deeply*

*—Plant a seed in a pot, water it, and observe the seed sprout and grow. Maybe you can nurture the plant to become a tree that will outlive you*

*—Visit a cave that has ancient paintings and ponder the motivations and the spirituality of the people who painted it. Check if you need permission, first*

*—Learn about climate change and then sit in quiet contemplation of this knowledge until you feel it*

*—Go to a place where wildlife congregates and try to be accepted as a witness*

# A Sustainable Life Philosophy

*—Meet with your local Indigenous clan and learn about their spiritual connection to the land*

*—Visit a waterfall and sit in quiet contemplation with the sound of the falling water*

*—Ponder the Gaia Hypothesis, how life on Earth maintains the atmosphere to keep conditions suited to life. Then, contemplate how much of an aberration it is that one species —Homo sapiens—could risk most life on Earth by fostering climate and ecological collapse.*

*—Ask yourself, what is important to me. What should I do with the rest of my life?*

# Imagine Reflourishing

Around the world, pretty much every major ecosystem has been mismanaged by human hands. Where these was once an abundance of life, clear waters or dense forest, there is now a lifeless wasteland, contaminated with agricultural chemicals or scarred by fire.

Vita Sapien

This abject situation is caused by the widespread adoption of denatured spiritualities.

This is not how it ought to be, and it is time to put it right through a global mass-movement to adopt and practice Ecosystem Spirituality, or something like it.

The help get this movement going, Vita Sapien asks you to imagine a world where these ecosystems are restored allowing for the beauty and wonder of nature to prosper and flourish as it once did before.

The story the Aral Sea demonstrates that major ecosystems can be brought back to full health.

At 68,000 km?, the Aral Sea was once the third-largest lake in the world. It began shrinking in the 1960s after the Soviet Union diverted the rivers feeding it to irrigate vast cotton and rice fields. By 2007, it had declined

# A Sustainable Life Philosophy

to just 10% of its original size and the exposed seabed became a toxic salt desert.

In recent years, however, strategic efforts have been made to restore the ecological integrity of the Aral Sea. There has been dramatic success in some quarters.

Restoring damaged ecosystems of this scale is hugely complicated and can take many years. But it is possible if enough people are motivated and committed to the long haul.

No matter which country you are from, there is a large-scale ecosystem needing a commitment expedient effort.

In Iran—for example—the massive saltwater Lake Urmia is suffering catastrophic collapse in its ecosystem, a parched lakebed devoid of life. Imagine the reflourishing of Lake Urmia, the water returned and the lake a rippling sea of pink flamingo, safe in the knowledge that there lays an abundant source of artemia shrimp for food. If you are in Iran, get your head around the politics of Lake Urmia and then get to work doing what is necessary to fix it.

In Iraq, imagine the iconic Mesopotamian Marshes at the confluence of the Tigris and Euphrates being bought back to life.

In Australia, imagine the great forests are protected and the koala population is growing steadily. Imagine the reflourishing of Murray Darling river and the Great Barrier Reef no-longer a risk of bleaching. Imagine Ningaloo reef and the whale sharks no longer at risk from seismic exploration or oil spills.

In Brazil, imagine the reflourishing of the Atlantic Forest—once covering the entire coast from north to south, now reduced to fragments. Picture the golden lion tamarins swinging through restored canopy, the jaguar prowling protected corridors, and indigenous communities stewarding ancestral lands once again.

# A Sustainable Life Philosophy

Imagine Ma Ganga—the Ganges River, sacred to a billion Hindus—cleaned of faecal coliform bacteria and chromium contamination that chokes its middle regions. Imagine Ma Ganga heaving with healthy aquatic life from the headwaters in the Himalayas to the Sundarbans on the coast.

In the Sundarbans spanning coastal India and Bangladesh imagine the reflourishing of the world's largest tidal forest that is home to Royal Bengal tigers who watch over the carbon safely stored in estuarine sediments.

On the Fiji Islands, imagine the restoration of the great cedar and kauri forests that have been ruthlessly stripped by logging companies since colonial times.

It is all too easy to assume that the way things are is how they ought to be. Often, people in power will spread this belief in order to maintain their position.

Reimagining is not a call to try and get an exact copy of what was there before, as nature exists in so many various forms. Nor is it a call to exclude humans from these areas, but to restore the broad ecological function in a way that embraces the best of humanity.

Remember also that all ecosystems are threatened with extinction from climate change. So, no place is safe while the fossil fuel industry remains a dominant force in the world.

# Renaturing Religion

While five in eight humans follow a religion and the biosphere is collapsing, one might say that religions aren't all that good at nurturing the Living Planet.

World religions lack autopoiesis—a self-preservation mechanisms that would encourage the protection of the global ecosystem on which practitioners depend.

# A Sustainable Life Philosophy

There is, after-all, no religion on a dead planet —and that is exactly where we are headed absent a transformative shift in the relationship between humans and the Living Planet. Religions can help.

Every major religious tradition contains both the seeds of ecological consciousness (creation myth) and the seeds of ecological destruction (End Times myth). If religions are to have a meaningful role to play in advancing the Verdant Age, the responsibility falls on practitioners to cultivate one and starve the other.

For Christians, Creation Care offers an interpretation of scripture that emphasizes caring for that which their God is said to have created, viewing environmental stewardship as a sacred duty.

In Islam is the concept of Khalifa (stewardship)—humans as caretakers of Earth, not owners. The Islamic Foundation for Ecology and Environmental Sciences teaches that all creation is sacred trust from Allah, and destroying nature violates Islamic law.

In Judaism, the concept of Tikkun Olam — repairing the world — calls practitioners to active restoration of what has been broken, including and especially the Living Planet.

In Hinduism is a tradition of ancient nature worship—rivers as goddesses (Ma Ganga), trees as sacred (Peepal, Banyan), animals as divine manifestations.

Socially Engaged Buddhism emphasises interbeing—the radical interconnection of all life. In this tradition, compassion for all sentient beings extends without boundary, from the monastery to the forest and beyond.

Adapting religious teachings to the environmental challenges of the day may require a radical re-reading of the sacred texts as they were written long before there was a

## A Sustainable Life Philosophy

climate and ecological crisis—indeed before climate and ecology were even words.

This is an inherently logical thing to do, to protect your own life support system. Plus, why would a supreme being go to all the trouble of creating a beautiful biosphere only to have believers mess it up a few thousand years later?

If enough people can imagine reflourishing and take expedient, we will be underway with the transition to the Verdant Age.

# The Transition

## The Verdant Age

The Verdant Age is a potential future time when human civilization and the Living Planet thrive in synergy. Let's break that down because it is important.

- Thrive suggests not just surviving but prospering.
- In synergy means that each party is better off with the other.

The concept of the Verdant Age is not just wishful thinking but is consistent with scientific frameworks such as:

## A Sustainable Life Philosophy

- Gaia 2.0
- Class-5 (Agency Dominated) Planets
- Earth System Stewardship
- Ecozoic Era
- Ecological Civilization

One might ask, how long could the Verdant Age last?

A year, as we all know, is the time it takes for our planet Earth to orbit the Sun. What is less well known is that our solar system is entrained within the Milky Way Galaxy that rotates around its galactic core every 230 million years or so. This is referred to as a Galactic Year.

Vita Sapien Philosophy holds that the Verdant Age could last a Galactic Year. This means that humans could be living happily on Earth more than 200 million years from now.

Advancing the Verdant Age so that human civilization might survive a Galactic Year is the *raison d'etre* of Vita Sapien Philosophy.

## Vita Sapien

A nice aspiration, indeed, but if you chart the current trajectory of human civilization, you will see that we are heading rapidly towards the abyss. If we are to enter the Verdant Age, we need to change trajectory.

To reach the Verdant Age, it is necessary to swiftly change the trajectory of human civilization and resolve the Anthropocene Crisis with enough of the Living Planet intact, and a high-enough proportion of people with Ecosystem Spirituality.

By necessity, a sustainable civilization will have sustainable levels of population and consumption and if we have learned anything from the Anthropocene, it is where the limits lie.

To achieve this in the narrow window of time remaining, the widespread uptake of a sustainable life philosophy grounded in nature spirituality is required.

# A Sustainable Life Philosophy

Remember that 80% of the world's energy comes from the fossil fuel industry, and the super-wealthy corporations, families, individuals and their enablers have zero intention of protecting the global ecosystem whilst they are gorging themselves from the multi-trillion-dollar fossil fuel trough.

These are the agents of the hyperthreat, and the business model of the elite is to continue growing the global economy based on fossil fuels. That's it.

We need to mercifully euthanise the fossil fuel industry before it mercilessly kills us all. The sustainability crisis is a crisis of power. They wield it effectively. We don't. Yet.

Transitioning to a sustainable future requires overthrowing the destructive systems of power that exist on Earth today. This will require a herculean effort that only a spiritual motivation can provide. To get a frame of reference of how bad things could get, we can look back in time to the Permian Extinction.

# Changing Trajectory

Our civilization is entrained in the deadly rapids that get more dangerous as we continue blindly on. As the global economy grows at around 3% per annum, so does its energy metabolism and its toxic waste by-products.

Around 80% of the global economy's energy comes from fossil fuels, and humanity spews around 50 billion tons of heat-trapping carbon dioxide pollution into the atmosphere every year. In addition, we hack-down, chop-up, rip-out, obliterate, annihilate, and poison the global ecosystem, our life support.

We get closer to the precipice every day, and we are now in the final few years of maintaining agency over our destiny. No person in their right mind wants to live through global ecological collapse. And yet, we are all part of the cause and the consequence of this situation. Fortunately, there is an alternative.

# A Sustainable Life Philosophy

The alternative is to change trajectory and restore the global biosphere to full health.

**Vita Transition Plan**

This can be advanced by completing the Vita Transition Plan:

- Climate Reset
- Wild Revival
- Planet Detox
- Circular Future
- Nature First

Let's consider each of these elements recognising that they are not in chronological order and should all be attempted simultaneously.

- **Climate Reset:** Transition away from fossil fuels to the efficient use of sustainable, clean energy, and safely drawdown 1 trillion tons of $CO_2$ to restore the climate to how it was before the industrial revolution

- **Wild Revival:** nurture endangered species back to stable populations, and re-wild a third or more of the planet to restore biosphere integrity

- **Planet Detox:** Transform the waste left behind by 250 years of industrial civilization including landfills, marine plastics, chemical and nuclear waste

- **Circular Future:** Create a fair and efficient, ecologically sustainable global socioeconomic system so that all humans can thrive

- **Nature First:** Foster a spiritual and intellectual bond to nature in all cultures to ensure that we don't end up at the brink of the abyss again

# A Sustainable Life Philosophy

In addition to cleaning up the mess we have made, we humans might be useful to the biosphere in unique ways.

Humans provide the biosphere with a threat management capability, i.e. looking out for Earth-killing asteroids, and destroying or deflecting them.

Humans could conceivably help the biosphere to reproduce by taking Earth species to another part of the solar system and thereby extending the life of Earth biota beyond the Long Future.

Hold-up, Mars enthusiasts, I know you are aching to colonise Mars, but we shouldn't even be thinking about going to other planets until the home planet Earth is brought back to full health.

That is a form of civilisation discipline that we need to learn.

## Vita Sapien

Finally, a poetic benefit: humans give the biosphere consciousness, a capacity for self-awareness.

It was, after-all, humans who in 1968 took the first Biosphere Selfie, the famous Earthrise photo from the Apollo-8 mission. It wasn't the dolphins or white mice that took that photo, we did.

One could argue the benefits of a biosphere being aware of itself, but as components of the biosphere, we humans gain a deeper understanding of ourselves from Biosphere Selfies. By seeing Earth from space, we gain a perspective we don't have in our daily lives.

The first Earth Selfie was black and white with the Moon in the foreground. A few minutes later the iconic, colour Earthrise photo was taken.

Today, there is a satellite positioned at a location in space called L1 that provides a daily Earth Selfie. You can see these images

## A Sustainable Life Philosophy

on the website. Just google DSCOVR: EPIC. While you are looking at these amazing photos, consider how you can get involved in the transition to the Verdant Age and engage in Vita Practice.

# Vita Practice

## Fostering Mass-Ecophany

While it is innate for humans to be in tune with nature, not everyone is.

One of Vita Sapien Philosophy's unique ideas is called *ecophany*, or *ecological epiphany*.

This is an emotional, spiritual, or intellectual awakening to nature.

Ecophany is a one-way street because once you sense what humans have done to our Living Planet and what the planet is soon to do to us, you can't unfeel it. It changes your life. You will find yourself reconsidering

# A Sustainable Life Philosophy

everything that you previously thought was important, and your behaviour will change.

Ecophany is emotionally challenging, but it is a necessary pathway to enlightenment: *understanding how things really are*.

Fostering Ecophany involves creating conditions suited to helping people experience ecophany. To this end, programs can be developed that invite people to open their hearts to nature and our Living Planet.

*You've had your coffee,
but have you had ecophany?*

Mass-Ecophany is the concept of ecophany occurring in tens of millions of people. So, Fostering Mass-Ecophany is ultimately what

# Vita Sapien

Vita Sapien Philosophy seeks to achieve. And given the urgency of our climate and ecological crisis, Fostering Rapid Mass-Ecophany is what we need to do. But that is not enough.

A spiritual enlightenment is like hoisting a huge spinnaker sail on a yacht. What's also needed is a rudder to set the direction of the vessel, a chart, and a plan of how to get to a desired destination.

All these ideas can be brought together in programs that include the following elements:

- Spiritual enlightenment to nature
- Understanding the Earth System
- A map for the future (Transition)
- A destination (the Verdant Age)
- Duties for the crew to achieve the mission (Earthwork)

To prevent the collapse of the global ecosystem, we need a powerful spiritual enlightenment to nature for hundreds of

## A Sustainable Life Philosophy

millions of people around the world, framed by environmental science and directed towards expedient action.

Then, there is hope that humanity may enter the Verdant Age that will extend deep into the Long Future. To achieve the Verdant Age, we need action. The following chapter helps explain what needs to happen in the transition to the Verdant Age.

When people have had ecophany, they are primed to take action that is referred to as Earthwork.

# Earthwork

Earthwork describes the duties that we can all undertake to bring about the transition to the Verdant Age.

If our civilization is to survive, we need to make this transition swift and effective: *Full Transition, full-speed ahead*. If we just do Partial Transition, so much will be lost that we will risk losing it all. If we continue the way we are going– Zero Transition–*Homo sapiens* face oblivion along with most of the plants and creatures on our beautiful Living Planet.

The purpose of Earthwork is to make collapse as shallow as possible and resolve the Anthropocene Crisis in a single human generation.

Humans arrived on Earth through the same evolutionary pathway as the trees, the bees, the whales, and the snails. As such, we have the same responsibilities to the Living Planet: to pursue our own interests in a manner that supports the well-being of the whole.

An enabler of Earthwork is a spiritual connection to our Living Planet. With this spiritual enlightenment, you are empowered to contribute to advancing the Verdant Age. The Vita Quests can guide you in these actions.

A Sustainable Life Philosophy

# Vita Quests

Vita Quests are actions that anyone can undertake to help transition to the Verdant Age.

1. I, Biosphere
2. Live with Earthity
3. Practice a Vitamission
4. Grow Something
5. Find Yourself in Nature
6. Celebrate the Moon
7. Cosmos & Magma
8. Know Your Boundaries
9. Embrace the Storm
10. Reinvent New Year
11. Know Your White Horse
12. Return to the Flux

# I, Biosphere

We are all part of the biosphere, and the biosphere is part of us. The acceptance of this idea is called *I, Biosphere*.

We wouldn't be here if it wasn't for the biosphere, so every-day, in some way, say thanks or take some time to connect-in with nature.

If you are in a big hurry, maybe just say "Thanks Plankton" as a way of recognising the wonderful things that the biosphere provides for us.

Maybe say "Hi" to a cloud or shake the leaves of a tree.

Feel free to create your own *I, Biosphere* routine and share with others. The more we acknowledge, connect to, and give thanks to our Living Planet, the more we realise that we just can't live without her.

# A Sustainable Life Philosophy

There is a simple I, Biosphere poem that you might like to recite as a way of confirming that you identify as part of the biosphere.

*I am human, I come from Earth*

*In a little bubble of gas*

*With molten magma below*

*The freezing depths of space above*

*I am one organism*

*Made of billions of organisms*

*Amongst trillions of organisms*

*In a vibrant community*

*A biological sphere of life*

*The biosphere*


*I am part of the biosphere*

## Vita Sapien

*I, biosphere*

*You, also, are part of the biosphere*

*You, biosphere*

*We are all in this together*

*The humans and all else that lives on Earth*

*We, biosphere*

*We are all part of the biosphere*

*And the biosphere is part of us*

*So, we should care for the biosphere*

*We really can't live without her*

This short poem could become part of an initiation ritual into a Vita Pod, which is a group of people who put Vita Sapien Philosophy into practice.

A Sustainable Life Philosophy

# Live with Earthity

The name Vita Sapien is roughly translated from Latin to 'Life Wise'. Life wise has two connotations:

- Wise about our personal life
- Wise about our place amongst life on Earth

While much of Vita Sapien Philosophy is concerned with our personal relationship with the biosphere, it is through Earthity that we deal with personal and interpersonal issues. Earthity has three components:

- Live Lightly on the Earth
- Be Kind to Others
- Be Kind to Yourself

**Live Lightly on the Earth**

As cells in the body of Gya, we have common responsibilities to our fellow cells, and that means to other people and to nature. Vita

Sapien Philosophy calls upon people to be good neighbours and good environmentalists.

Western lifestyles are unsustainable because the dominant social, political and economic systems and their use of energy and materials are pushing us beyond safe planetary boundaries. With that said, it is relatively easy to slash one's material and energy consumption through conscious consumption and this should be done as a matter of course. This book does not delve into the details of Live Lightly on the Earth because it is so well covered elsewhere, for example, google 'sustainable lifestyles' to get started.

**Kind to Others**

Living with Earthity also means being decent to people who are and aren't like you. You can be anything, so be kind. Don't hate people. Don't be racist, homophobic, transphobic, misogynistic, sociopathic, etc.

# A Sustainable Life Philosophy

So many of the world's problems are caused by people who simply aren't kind to other people. Thieves, murderers, rapists, and abusers of men, women and children fit into this category. Many people are bought up around violence and use violence as a daily tool. Rise above this. The word *'sapiens'* means wise. So, use wisdom to defuse conflicts.

*Kind to Others* calls upon us to be okay with the lifestyles of people who aren't like you. If you don't like the idea of gay marriage, that's fine, don't marry a homosexual. If drug taking offends you, that's fine, don't take drugs.

Vita Sapien Philosophy holds that people ought to be free to live their lives without others interfering because their moral values sit in judgement. If people just let other people live their lives, everyone could just get on with living their lives.

With this said, the *Tolerance Paradox* tells us that if we want to live in a tolerant society, we need to be intolerant to intolerant people. A tolerant society must be prepared to defend itself against fascists and Nazis.

On the matter of war, it is accepted that sometimes war is a necessary pursuit, for example to repel an invading force. However, there is nonetheless a need for that war to be just and to be fought justly. Wars where soldiers attack soldiers are bad enough without soldiers abusing civilians or captives.

*Kind to Others* may seem simple and straightforward, but there are some nuances. As an example, there are training courses that help people identify racism and sexism in their behaviour that they may not have seen, themselves. In addition, there is a field called *non-violent communication* that similarly helps people communicate in a non–confrontational manner. *Kindness to Others* calls on people to familiarise themselves with these things and bring them into practice through their lives.

Many spiritual traditions promote charitable giving as a way of sharing the bounty that comes to an individual and help ameliorate social problems caused by systemic wealth disparity. Vita Sapien Philosophy condones this and accepts that changing the system that creates wealth disparity is the ultimate resolution of the problem. Charitable donations ought to be considered with reference to the concept of 'expedience'. This suggests that we ought to seek to do as much good with the donation as possible.

## Kind to Yourself

While we live surrounded by other people who engage in reciprocity and cooperation, at the end of the day we were born alone, and we die alone. In between, there are many decisions that are made that either advance our personal interests or run counter to them. Being kind to yourself is important.

*Kind to Yourself* covers the whole spectrum of what is referred to as Personal Development which includes personal finances, plus health and fitness, mental health, and so on.

## Vita Sapien

Avoiding harmful addictions is a part of Kind to Yourself.

Regarding wealth creation, it is important to consider how wealth is made and how it is consumed. For an example, someone who makes money from oil exploration (in a climate crisis) and spends his money shooting elephants (in a biodiversity crisis) ought never earn another dollar. On the other extreme, someone who makes money advancing sustainable energy and spends their money advancing noble causes, ought rightly do well for themselves.

## Practice a Vitamission

Every cell in a body is tasked with a specific mission. So, it is with us humans, except that we have agency, which means that we can choose our own mission.

What is your self-chosen mission to help Advance the Verdant Age?

# A Sustainable Life Philosophy

Given that climate change and biodiversity are the two biggest threats to the Living Planet, these might be the primary focus of your attention.

There are many ways to support our Living Planet including removing plastic from beaches, climate activism, developing new technology, or researching who's responsible for bad governance and holding them accountable. However, supporting environmental efforts should not come at the expense of human well-being, and vice-versa.

Ideally, a cause could foster more than one benefit. For example, supporting women to plant trees in developing countries helps to eradicate poverty, sequester carbon, and improve biodiversity.

Seek to make your Vitamission as impactful as possible and seek to continually increase your efficacy. This is referred to as expedience.

Devote your life to your Vitamission and become a powerful force in the transition to a sustainable global civilization.

## Grow Something

Growing something helps to connect people to Gya and the life-force that drives organisms to prosper. If you are not familiar with growing things, maybe start with a Swiss Cheese Plant – *Monstera deliciosa*. To get started, find someone who has a Monstera and ask for a cutting.

You might also take an interest in a home aquarium or a frog pond in the backyard. Frog ponds are good as they can enhance local ecosystems. Maybe combine the Monstera deliciosa with the frog pond.

In this way, you can connect directly to the wellbeing of other organisms and learn how to make them comfortable. If plants are comfortable, they grow and flower. If fish are comfortable, they breed.

## A Sustainable Life Philosophy

While you can grow things yourself, you can also participate in growing things with others. Collective actions can help restore entire ecosystems, forests and marine environments. The *Vita Transition Plan* calls for the rewilding of vast tracks of Earth, that is a growing mission you can get involved in.

## Find Yourself in Nature

Periodically immerse yourself in nature. Ideally, you would find a place where the technosphere is absent. No roads, and no traffic noise. It's hard to escape aeroplane noise, however.

If you can't escape a city, then go to the botanical gardens, or some place that is overgrown.

Immersing yourself in nature helps reconnect you to wilderness, a sensation that has been largely lost through urbanisation.

In Japan, there is a practice called *Shinrin-yoku or Forest Bathing*. This involves visiting a forest and engaging with nature through through all five senses. There is a large body of medical research that demonstrates the benefits for health through relaxation and stress reduction from being in nature.

There is another aspect to finding yourself in nature: nature helps you *find yourself*.

It helps you become present to your *Inner Self*. This is why it is important sometimes to be alone in nature, to discover yourself outside of someone else's frame of reference.

# Celebrate the Moon

On the Full Moon, gather with friends and associates and use this auspicious event to engage in an evening of Big Talk. A gathering on the Full Moon has several key attributes.

### A Peak Experience

The rise of the Full-Moon provides a peak experience in nature – the Moon Illusion. The Moon Illusion is an optical illusion that makes

# A Sustainable Life Philosophy

the Moon appear larger near the horizon than it does higher in the sky.

## Joins Us Together

The Moon is a great leveller of humans as it joins us together across space and time. The Moon looks the same, no matter where we are.

A Full Moon in Malaysia occurs on the same night as a Full Moon in Australia, for example.

The Moon has looked the same to all humans over the entire course of human history. So, when Shakespeare wrote *"The Moon's an arrant thief, and her pale fire she snatches from the sun,"* he was referring to the Moon that looked the same as the Moon that we see today.

## Reminder of Life

The Moon offers a visible reminder that we do not just live in a constructed society, but we are part of an ancient natural system that has been here long before us. The Moon is dead, inert, and lifeless, reminding us that life is the exception, not the rule, in our solar system.

The Moon has a huge influence on living things as its gravity moves trillions of tonnes of seawater around, causing the rise and fall of the tides. The Full Moon floods the night with light, making landscapes and seascapes visible in the dark.

So, every time you see the Moon think of life on Earth and how precious it is.

**Renewable Energy**

The tides, caused by the influence of the Moon's gravity, can be harnessed to provide clean renewable energy. The Moon thus reminds us of the need to end the fossil fuel industry and advance sustainable renewable energy.

A Sustainable Life Philosophy

## Cosmos & Magma

According to the 2016 paper, The New World Atlas of Artificial Night Sky Brightness, about 30% of humans will never see the Milky Way from their homes due to night sky light pollution.

Seeing the cosmos reminds us that Earth is a planet of one star (the Sun), amid trillions of stars in a vast expanding bubble of vacuous space. This is where we live, and to see the stars of our galaxy, the Milky Way, on a clear night serves to remind us of the frailty of our blue/green planet.

What lies above the biosphere is a vast expanse of space that is a frigid -273 degree Celsius. Not a welcoming environment for life.

To manifest this contemplation, visit a place where artificial night sky brightness is minimal or zero to view the cosmos. You will need a map for this. A skyglow map. So, google Skyglow Map.

You might also contemplate what lies below the Living Planet. What lies below the biosphere is a bubbling cauldron of molten rock – the magma – at a temperature of around 1,000 degrees Celsius.

This contemplation might be advanced by visiting a volcano. However, there is an ecological footprint to travel (consider your Earthity), and volcanoes can be dangerous; so, one might simply ponder volcanoes and magma through a book, a website, or a documentary.

Alternatively, visit hot springs. This is where water is heated by magma and finds its way to the surface. There are many hot springs around the world, some that you can bathe in.

Maybe you can find hot springs that are in a place with zero skyglow and contemplate what lies above and below the biosphere at the same time.

There is a takeaway message in these contemplations of the Cosmos and the Magma. The biosphere has dangerous neighbours and yet can maintain internal temperatures within a narrow range despite the extremes of temperature on either side. We ought not tamper with that ability.

## Know Your Boundaries

Know Your Boundaries is a call to develop Earth Consciousness by learning how our planet provides us with a life support system. The scientific field called Planetary Boundaries is discussed earlier in this book. You can learn about the Planetary Boundaries through reading and watching videos. In addition, you can go and visit places to help you learn. For example, visit the local dams, lakes and rivers to learn about Planetary Boundary: Freshwater. Go somewhere you can see a fossil fuel power station and a wind farm to get a better understanding of the human influence on the climate system.

## Embrace the Storm

Embrace the storm has three meanings.

First, take the opportunity to experience heavy weather when it comes, to get a deeper connection with nature. Stand in the rain, feel the strong breeze on your skin. Visit the site of a flood to develop a deeper understanding of how weather systems influence your region.

Second, seek a deeper understanding of meteorology, the science of the weather. Learn how clouds form and why storms do what they do. This will help give you advanced warning of extreme weather. Pay special attention when large weather systems are approaching, and use these instances to share your knowledge with others and learn from what they know.

Third, find inner-peace with the understanding that we have destabilised

# A Sustainable Life Philosophy

Earth's climate, and extreme weather is coming to us all, eventually.

As we continually add 50 billion tons of greenhouse gas into the atmosphere, we heat the planet plus increase the amount of water vapour in the atmosphere. We are heading into an age of storms that will get worse and worse until we overthrow the destructive systems of power, resolve the Anthropocene, and enter the Verdant Age.

## Reinvent New Year

At the heart of this practice is the recognition that all institutions are ecologically unsustainable and must be transformed to advance the Verdant Age.

The term institution includes a wide range of entities, practices and norms that structure social life such as banking, finance, energy production, governance, public holidays – including New Years. All institutions need augmentation to align with a sustainable civilization.

Vita Sapien Organisation has taken up this challenge and reinvented New Year away from the 1st of January.

A New Year is an arbitrary date, after all. When is the natural beginning and end of an orbit around the sun? There isn't one. So, around the world, cultures ascribe different dates to the beginning of the New Year.

Vita Sapien Philosophy believes that it is auspicious to celebrate New Year on a date that advances the conversation about the Living Planet and the Verdant Age. As such Vita Sapien Organisation's Foundation Pod celebrates New Year on 16 July. The minute of the end of one annual cycle and the beginning of the next is 9.29pm Australian Eastern Standard Time (AEST).

At that time in 1945 in New Mexico, USA, the first nuclear explosion was detonated: the

# A Sustainable Life Philosophy

so-called Alamogordo Bomb Test. This event is significant because radioactive contamination from atmospheric bomb tests has been identified as a potential chemical marker of the beginning of the Anthropocene Epoch, and this was the first such bomb test.

Vita Sapien Philosophy holds that the New Mexico nuclear bomb test as the beginning of the Anthropocene Epoch.

Every year Vita Sapien's Foundation Pod holds a New Year celebration on 16 July.

At 9.29pm AEST, the Gadget is primed then detonated, creating a small explosion created from dry-ice in a soft drink bottle submerged in a bucket of water with a bright LED light shining behind.

When the Gadget detonates, it shoots a bubbling plume of aerated water into the air accompanied by a loud *POP!* The LED light illuminates the bubbles as a bright white flash. This ceremony is called *Trinibomtess* and commemorates the beginning of the New Year.

It is fitting to align the Earth New Year with the beginning of the Anthropocene Epoch, as Vita Sapien Philosophy seeks to help foster the creation of a subsequent era where humans thrive in synergy with nature. We refer to this subsequent epoch as the Verdant Age. The sooner that starts, the better.

Commemorating the first nuclear bomb test is appropriate because there are many prognostications about the world ending in fire due to Climate Change, Armageddon, Nuclear War, etc. These ideas are widespread in Western culture and religious traditions. It is therefore refreshing to find a narrative in which the fireball occurs at the beginning of the story, leaving the end-date for humanity to be decided deep into the Long Future.

Vita Pods (groups of people who practice Vita Sapien Philosophy) are invited to accept Foundation Pod's New Year date or to propose their own. The choice of their New Year needs to be backed by a rational justification of how this date helps to advance the Verdant Age.

Remember, that the exhortation to Reinvent New Years is a call to reinvent all institutions, which includes but is not limited to banking, government, archery, netball, fishing, war, air travel…. All institutions should be reinvented to advance the Verdant Age.

## Know your White Horse

The Uffington White Horse is a Bronze-age artwork etched into a hillside in Oxfordshire, UK that is regarded as sacred by many people.

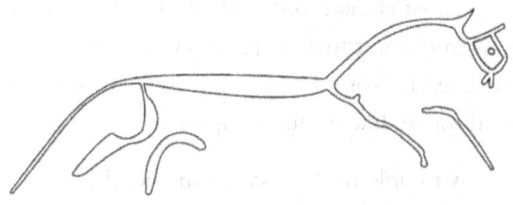

## Vita Sapien

*The Uffington White Horse is an iconic Bronze Age symbol on the side of a hill in the UK.*

Every year, thousands of people visit the White Horse to remove weeds, cut the grass, and add new chalk. The horse is elevated, giving a commanding view over the Oxfordshire landscape.

The practice *Know Your White Horse* is not an exhortation to visit the Uffington chalk-figure *per se* but represents whatever or wherever an individual goes for spiritual renewal through ritual in nature. If you do not know how to find spiritual renewal through ritual in nature, this is your next adventure.

Our civilisation is heading into a pressure cooker of climate and ecological collapse, and it is important that we all know how to regenerate from the battles that we choose and those that are thrust upon us.

Many people find solace on the beach, walking by the lake or watching the Full Moon rise. Spiritual solace in nature needn't

## A Sustainable Life Philosophy

be outside. A balcony full of pot-plants will do the trick for some. If you are unable to escape the bounds of the city, nature-spiritual solace can be found online, maybe watching videos of fish schooling or some such.

## Return to the Flux

Our bodies are the receptacles of minerals and energy borrowed from the Living Planet. When we die, we ought to promptly return the energy and minerals to the Living Planet so that other life forms might get the benefit of them.

This might be done through cremation, being aware of not using fossil fuels, or plastics in the casket. Alternatively, one might be buried in a casket that allows the soil to absorb the body easily.

There are various 'Green Funeral' practices that you might consider. This might include a simple practice like burial in a forest with a tree planted on your grave. There are more complex technological decomposition processes such as the system called *Recompose*.

When the minerals in your body return to the biochemical flux from where they came, you are contributing to the growth of new life. Who knows what living organisms may come to be the beneficiary of the minerals that you once were composed of?

This is the principle of Revitalisation. A Vitan funeral will help add new life to that which was once part of you.

Today, the average life expectancy of humans is about 72 years, ranging from 84 years in Japan to 54 years in the country of Chad in Africa. That's all you get. And that's all you need. One can do extraordinary things in just 54 years.

You were unalive for billions of years, you have a short time of being alive, and then you become unalive for billions more years. That's

## A Sustainable Life Philosophy

just how it is on Earth for all the animals and plants, humans included.

So, let us embrace being alive in the full knowledge that it doesn't last long. And similarly, let us embrace death as an inevitable conclusion to our brief time alive. And it is not just humans who have this fate, this is common to all that lives on Earth. Indeed, this is the fate of life itself, on Earth.

Life formed on Earth around 3.8 billion years ago in a process called abiogenesis, and will likely remain for another 2 billion years, beyond which time the Red Giant will swallow Earth, consuming all life. There are no formal names for the first living organisms, nor the prospective last ones to survive the Red Giant. So, we will create some names here. The first living organism we'll call *Bioprima*, and the last, *Biofinalis*.

Between Bioprima and Biofinalis is Earthlife that lasts about 6 billion years. You get to enjoy your 50 – 80 years during that time.

## Vita Sapien

When you become unalive, that which you leave behind is your Exosomatic Spirit. This might express through fond memories in the minds of the people who survive you.

If you invented a gadget, the existence of these gadgets is a part of your Exosomatic Spirit. If you planted a forest, the trees are a part of your spirit.

A Sustainable Life Philosophy

# Being Vitan

A Vitan is a person with three key traits:

- A spiritual bond to our Living Planet
- Trust in science and a grasp of reality
- In action to make things better

There are millions of Vitans in the world today. Some are atheist, some hold religious belief. Some are spiritual, some are not.

Throughout history, halos have represented enlightenment. From Jesus to Buddha, from Hindu deities to Islamic prophets, the halo signifies one who has achieved deeper understanding of reality.

Those who undergo ecophany—spiritual and intellectual awakening to our Living Planet—possess a form of enlightenment deserving recognition.

## Vita Sapien

The **Vitan Halo**, formed from the Quenn symbol (see next chapter), marks this ecological enlightenment: understanding that we are not separate from nature, but cells in the Living Planet.

We come from different countries, faiths and walks of life. We are united by our commitment to do what is necessary to transition to the Verdant Age and foster a sustainable global economy and a caring, nurturing society for the wellbeing of humanity and the Living Planet.

Just as traditional halos mark spiritual transcendence, the Vitan Halo marks ecological enlightenment: understanding that we are not separate from nature, but integral parts of the living biosphere.

Vitans exist across all walks of life—parents and engineers, teachers and executives, artists and scientists. The enlightenment manifests differently in each context, but the core understanding remains: we are cells in the body of Gya, the Living Planet.

## A Sustainable Life Philosophy

Those who find meaning in Vita Sapien Philosophy may want to share it with others. Here are some ways you can share Vita Sapien Philosophy.

> Visit the Vita Sapien website and join the social media, and like, follow, and share.
>
> ...
>
> Host a Full Moon Party and talk about Vita Sapien Philosophy to your guests.
>
> ...
>
> Invite people around for lunch to share Vita Sapien Philosophy.
>
> ...
>
> Order a box of Vita Sapien pocketbooks and gift them to friends and family.
>
> ...

## Vita Sapien

> Maybe form a Pod, a local gathering, to undertake Vita Practices and share the message.

Pods are gatherings of Vita Sapiens and Vitans who practice Vita Sapien Philosophy together.

You don't have to be a rocket scientist to create a Pod, but you need to have a grasp of Vita Sapien Philosophy before you can share it competently.

How to form a pod:

> Learn about Vita Sapien Philosophy.
>
> ...
>
> Choose a name for your pod and map out some activities for members.
>
> ...
>
> An excellent way to get started is to host a Moon Party.

# A Sustainable Life Philosophy

...

Invite people to join you in undertaking the Planetary Quests.

...

Have conversations about Living with Earthity and how to add expedience to your Vitamission.

...

Organise a Cosmos Night and go where there is not skyglow so you can see the stars at night.

...

Help people connect emotionally, cerebrally, and spiritually to the Living Planet.

...

Become actively involved in the rebellion against extinction.

...

## Vita Sapien

> Create a safe-space for people to talk about solastalgia and ecogrief and to share their fears for the future.
>
> ...
>
> Wear a Quendant, and when people enquire about it, share Vita Sapien Philosophy.

A Quendant? What's a Quendant, you ask?

A Sustainable Life Philosophy

# Resources

## About ViSO

Vita Sapien Philosophy is advanced by Vita Sapien Organisation (ViSO), an Australian registered charity that innovates at the intersection of environmental science and ecological spirituality.

ViSO's mission is to advance the Verdant Age, the potential future time when humanity and the biosphere thrive in synergy, deep into the Long Future.

ViSO shares its ideas through the website—vitasapien.org—through social media, and through this pocketbook.

Vita Sapien Philosophy is the sustainable life philosophy at the heart of all of ViSO's work.

To spread Vita Sapien Philosophy far and wide, ViSO needs resources to function and grow.

An excellent way of demonstrating your support is by wearing a Quendant: a Quenn Pendant

# The Quenn

The Quenn is Vita Sapien's primary icon and the symbol for the Anthropocene, the modern era in which humans are the main drivers of change in the climate and environment.

Within the Quenn symbol is the Verda, the symbol of the Verdant Age.

# A Sustainable Life Philosophy

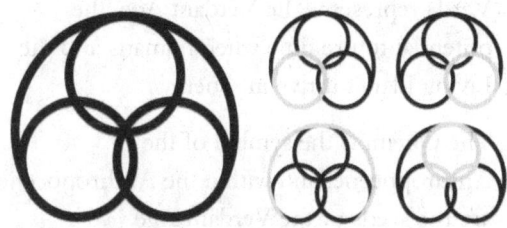

The Quenn symbol resonates with the Stockdale Paradox as it both asks us to accept reality (Anthropocene) and to hold faith in a possible future (Verdant Age).

In the Quenn symbol, the lower inner rings represent the Living Planet, and human civilisation, and the outer ring represents continuum, the ability to continue.

This outer ring is broken because human civilization is out of balance with the Living Planet—we've transgressed the Planetary Boundaries.

The upper, inner circle, incorporating the tops of the two lower circles, is the Verda symbol.

## Vita Sapien

Verda represents the Verdant Age, the potential future time when humans and the Living Planet thrive in synergy.

The Quenn is the symbol of the Anthropocene, and within the Anthropocene are the seeds of the Verdant Age.

A Quendant is a Quenn symbol worn as a pendant. These attractive jewellery pieces are produced by ViSO. The standard Quendant is made of laser-cut stainless steel with a stainless wire and magnetic clasp. They are a tried and tested piece of robust, attractive jewellery.

# A Sustainable Life Philosophy

If you wear a Quendant in public, people will comment on the piece, creating a space for a conversation about Vita Sapien Philosophy.

You can purchase Quendants through the Vita Sapien website where there are also Quendant explainer videos, and a lot of other merchandise.

If you want to help spread Vita Sapien Philosophy, you might consider a monthly donation to ViSO. That would help a lot.

Help Vita Sapien if you can. But what we most ask is that you is to pursue your life interest in a manner that makes a positive contribution to society and the Living Planet and advance the Verdant Age.

Learn more on the Vita Sapien website: vitasapien.org

# Glossary

**Advance the Verdant Age:** Undertake efforts to resolve the Anthropocene Crisis and advance a sustainable civilization where nature and humanity thrive in synergy, deep into the Long Future.

**Anthro:** Anthro is a prefix that describes humans.

**Anthropocene:** The Anthropocene is a central concept in Vita Sapien Philosophy that describes the modern era – since 1945 – in which humans are the main driver of change in the climate and environment.

**Anthropogenic:** Made by humans.

**Anthropogenic Mass:** The mass of material created by humans that since around the year

# A Sustainable Life Philosophy

2020 outweighs the mass of living things on Earth.

**Big Talk:** The opposite of small talk, Big Talk is conversations about substantial topics such as the climate and ecological crisis, human civilization, and the Verdant Age.

**Bio-physical Flux:** See Flux.

**Biosphere:** The biosphere has two meanings. First, it describes the thin-walled sphere where life can be found on Earth. Second, it refers to that place, and the totality of all the life found within it. Thus the biosphere is both a place and a thing.

**Cosmos Night:** A proposed activity to visit a location with zero skyglow at night during Milky Way season to view the full depth of the cosmos. This is part of developing a greater appreciation of what lies above Gya.

**Cro-Magnon:** The Cro-Magnon are the first *Homo sapiens* to arrive in Europe dating from

**Defaunation of the Anthropocene**: the past and future mass-death of animals in the modern era caused by direct and indirect human action.

**Earthity:** the practice of living lightly on Earth and caring for oneself and others.

**Earth New Year:** a Vitan New Year celebration on 16 July that commemorates the beginning of the Anthropocene.

**Ecophany:** formed from the words ecological and epiphany, ecophany is a core concept for Vita Sapien Philosophy and refers to a spiritual, emotional, or intellectual awakening to nature – and particularly the plight of the biosphere – in an individual. The mission of Vita Sapien Philosophy is to foster ecophany in hundreds of millions of people around the world, rapidly.

# A Sustainable Life Philosophy

**Euthanise the Fossil Fuel Industry:** to rapidly remove power of the fossil fuel industry to facilitate the rapid and swift and orderly transition to sustainable renewable energy.

**Expedience:** is like continual improvement, the idea that we should be constantly reframing our actions to make the as effective as possible.

**Flux:** the high-entropy environment of the ocean, atmosphere and soil from which low entropy structures are formed by plants. All that lives on Earth is comprised of flux.

**Fostering Rapid, Mass-Ecophany:** the process of swiftly fostering ecological epiphany in tens of millions of people worldwide.

**Gaia:** a name for Earth as a living planet derived from Gaia Theory, the concept that life on Earth behaves in the manner of an organism to maintain thermal equilibrium.

## Vita Sapien

**Gya:** the biosphere seen as a single living being, a spiritual belief fostered by Vita Sapien Philosophy.

**Holocene:** The Holocene Epoch is name given to the last 12,000 years since the retreat of the last Ice Age. During this period, humans went from being predominantly hunter-gatherers to developing agriculture, cities and towns, and so-called 'civilization'. Vita Sapien Philosophy teaches that the Holocene Epoch ended in the 1950s when the Anthropocene Epoch began.

**Long Future:** The Long Future refers to the vast stretch of time during which Earth remains habitable, thanks to its position within the Sun's Habitable Zone. This is the era when conditions allow life to thrive. However, as the Sun slowly ages and expands, Earth will eventually receive too much solar radiation. When that time comes, our planet's orbit will no longer support life—the

# A Sustainable Life Philosophy

temperatures will rise too high, and the biosphere will break down.

**Moon Party:** a gathering of Vitans to watch the Full Moon Rise and engage in Big Talk.

**Moonscope:** The practice of determining when and where the Full Moon rise will be visible. A good way to start is to google Full Moon Rise and the name of your city. If you land on timeanddate.com you are in a good place. You need to know the day, the time and the azimuth (compass direction).

**Nine-Boundaries Safe:** a design that helps ensure that none of the nine planetary boundaries are exceeded.

**Imperium:** Imperium is a word from Ancient Rome that describes an authority bestowed upon an individual to act with force on the behalf of the Roman Empire.

*Imperium vitae-planeta*: There are two aspects to the name *Imperium vitae-planeta*.

- *Imperium vitae-planeta* is a proposed taxonomic binomial (scientific name) for the biosphere as a single living being. Note the capitalisation and italics. The name roughly translates from Latin to Empire of the Living Planet.
-
- A second meaning of *Imperium vitae-planeta* is an intrinsic authority for humans to act with force of character on behalf of the Living Planet.

**Pod:** A Pod is a name ascribed to an organised gathering of individuals for the purpose of learning about, sharing and practicing Vita Sapien Philosophy.

**Proto-Vitan:** A person concerned about the climate and ecological crisis who is developing one or two of the three core Vitan characteristics: spiritual bond to nature, trust in science, and commitment to action.

# A Sustainable Life Philosophy

**Quenn:** A Vitan symbol that represents the Anthropocene.

**Quendant:** A Quenn Pendant, a Quenn symbol worn as a necklace. An iconic piece of Vitan jewellery.

**Resolve the Anthropocene**: This means to fix the climate and ecological crisis swiftly by euthanizing the fossil fuel industry, restoring the climate by drawing down a trillion tons of $CO_2$ and rewilding a third of nature. All this needs to be well underway by mid-century.

**Return to the Flux:** Vitan funerary practice seeks for the minerals and energy in a deceased individual to re-enter the flux from where it came thus enabling other living beings the opportunity to use those minerals and energy.

**Spiritual Renaturing:** The process of reconnecting human spirituality with the natural world, reversing the denaturation that occurred during the Axial Age. Spiritual

## Vita Sapien

Renaturing involves cultivating direct relationship with nature, embracing Ecosystem Spirituality, and allowing this transformed worldview to guide behaviour toward ecological restoration and sustainability.

**Technosphere:** the totality of all matter created by humans. It presently weighs more that the mass of the biosphere.

**Thrive in Synergy:** Thrive in synergy refers to the biosphere and human civilization prospering as a result of a synergistic interplay between the two. This is to say that the condition of the biosphere can be improved as a result of human actions.

**Uffington White Horse:** The Uffington White Horse is a horse-like symbol etched into the side of a hill in Southern England. The Uffington White Horse is the inspiration to the Vita Sapien Philosophy Practice, Know Your White Horse which describes knowing where to find spiritual solace in nature.

# A Sustainable Life Philosophy

**Verda:** a symbol that is derived from the Quenn that represents the Verdant Age.

**Verdant Age:** The Verdant Age is the potential future time when humans and the biosphere thrive in synergy deep into the Long Future.

*Vitae-planeta*: A shortened name for *Imperium vitae-planeta*, the biosphere of Planet Earth viewed as a single living organism. Note the capitalisation and spelling of *Vitae-planeta*, that is consistent with it being a species name.

**Vita Hypothesis:** the hypothesis that the combination of spiritual enlightenment to nature and environmental education is a pathway to fostering ecophany and triggering radical pro-environmental behaviour change.

**Vitan:** A person who has developed all three core characteristics: a spiritual bond to nature, trust in science and grasp of reality, and active commitment to making things better.

Vita Sapien

**Vita Sapien Organisation (ViSO):** is a registered charity in Australia that advances Vita Sapien Philosophy.

# About the Author

Guy Lane is a British-born Australian who makes his home in southeast Queensland. In his twenties, two years working in the offshore oil industry opened his eyes to the troubled relationship between humankind and the Living Planet. Seeking a truer path, he studied Environmental Science at Griffith University, living aboard his 34-foot yacht *Ophelia* on the Brisbane River and sailing the Queensland coast—a time in which he learned the ways of the Brown Booby bird,

# A Sustainable Life Philosophy

*Sula leucogaster*, and began to sense the subtle intelligence of nature.

In 2002, Guy founded SEAO2, a sustainability advisory firm. A decade later, while completing a Master of Business at QUT, he came to a profound realisation: that the climate and ecological crises are not merely technical failures, but symptoms of a deeper disorder—a flaw in the worldview and spirituality that drive civilization. He understood that his fascination with nature, and with the Brown Booby bird in particular, was not just admiration, but a spiritual affection. This was the seed of what would become *Vita Sapien Philosophy*.

In 2020, he established **Vita Sapien** as a registered charity. Over the next five years, he lived a humble, nomadic life from *Motel Prius*—his Gen 2 Toyota hatchback—researching and writing *Vita Sapien Philosophy*. During a journey to Bicheno, Tasmania, inspired by the southern ocean and the orange-lichened boulders, he wrote the first draft.

Much of the subsequent writing unfolded on a property on the Sunshine Coast, where Guy lived among Eastern Grey Kangaroos and the many gentle members of Australia's living world. It was there that the philosophy came fully alive — not as abstraction, but as reflection of the wonder of the biosphere.

**Guy Lane:** *"The Verdant Age is not a dream. It's a transformative idea whose time has come."*

# Contact ViSO

vitaeplaneta@gmail.com

# Comments From Readers

This is a Vita Sapien pass-around pocketbook.

Write your comments below and then give the book to someone, asking them to read the

# A Sustainable Life Philosophy

book, make a comment and pass it on to someone else.

Name: _____ Date: _____

Contact (optional): _____

Comment: _____

# Vita Sapien

# A Sustainable Life Philosophy

# Vita Sapien

# A Sustainable Life Philosophy

## Vita Sapien

# A Sustainable Life Philosophy

# Vita Sapien

www.ingramcontent.com/pod-product-compliance
Lightning Source LLC
Chambersburg PA
CBHW011129070526
44583CB00023B/2968